Techniques - Techniques - Techniques:

Play-Based Activities for Children, Adolescents, & Families

Sueann Kenney-Noziska, MSW, LCSW, RPT-S

ISBN 978-0-7414-4607-7

Published by:

1094 New Dehaven Street, Suite 100
West Conshohocken, PA 19428-2713
Info@buybooksontheweb.com
www.buybooksontheweb.com
Toll-free (877) BUY BOOK
Local Phone (610) 941-9999
Fax (610) 941-9959

Printed in the United States of America
Published October 2012

~ Dedication ~

This book is dedicated to the courageous children, adolescents, and families I have had the privilege and honor of knowing through the course of my clinical practice. Their perseverance and determination inspire me.

Acknowledgments

This book was inspired by the children, adolescents, and families I have had the honor and privilege of working with over the years. I would like to extend my appreciation and gratitude to my colleagues and supervisors at Riverside County Department of Mental Health for the clinical opportunities and professional collaboration I have received. In addition, a special acknowledgment goes to Liana Lowenstein, Janine Shelby, and DeeDee Ginns-Gruenberg for their input and guidance on this manuscript and the publication process. As this book became a reality, my deepest gratitude to my family and friends for their words of encouragement and support. Finally, to my husband, Robert J. Noziska, I am forever grateful for your unwavering dedication, inspiration, love, and patience.

Table of Contents

Introduction

Based on the need to continually incorporate new, clinically sound play therapy interventions into my practice, the techniques in this manual were created and this book came to fruition. Working with children, adolescents, and families in the mental health field can be a very rewarding, albeit challenging, endeavor. Clinical work with children, adolescents, and families who are struggling with mental health problems or facing psychosocial stressors demands competent intervention with an emphasis on approaches that are developmentally appropriate and effective. Play therapy provides a developmentally sensitive medium to address the needs of these populations. "Techniques-Techniques-Techniques" provides a variety of age-appropriate tools for clinical practice. Techniques contained in this manual can be utilized for an array of presenting problems and symptoms and are applicable across diverse treatment settings, modalities, and diagnoses. This book is written to serve as a resource for a variety of professionals, including counselors, social workers, clinical psychologists, school personnel, and other professionals who provide mental health services to children, adolescents, and families.

Techniques in this book focus on a variety of therapeutic issues and are divided into chapters based on different areas of clinical focus. Specific areas covered in this manual include Assessment and Engagement, Emotional Expression, Coping Skills, ADHD, Self-Esteem, Interpersonal Boundaries, Sexual Abuse, and Termination. Each technique is presented in a manner that supports easy integration into practice. Interventions are described with step-by-step instructions as well as information regarding the purpose of the technique, the age range and the modality the technique is best suited for. A listing of materials needed is also available. A "Resources and Materials" section is included at the back of this text to provide clinicians with potential vendors to purchase play therapy materials and supplies. In addition, a list of "Professional Associations & Resources" is presented to assist clinicians in their professional growth and development.

The interventions proposed in this book, though not empirically validated, have proven useful in practice based upon my own clinical experience and the anecdotal reports of clinicians who have utilized these activities. These techniques are intended to supplement sound, basic clinical training and can be modified as needed to meet the treatment needs of individual clients. As with most techniques, the interventions presented here are intended to be incorporated into a broader, clinically sound treatment approach and should not be used in isolation.

I have gained a tremendous wealth of knowledge from the children, adolescents, and families for whom these techniques and interventions have been developed for. I am hopeful you will find these tools helpful in your work as well.

Best wishes,

-Sueann Kenney-Noziska, MSW, LCSW, RPT-S

Considerations for Use

"Techniques-Techniques-Techniques" is a collection of creative, practical, play-based techniques to address the treatment needs of children and adolescents struggling with psychosocial difficulties or mental health problems. These techniques are intended to supplement clinically sound, theoretically grounded therapeutic work. The following issues are intended to support the integration of these tools into clinical practice.

The Therapeutic Relationship

The importance of the therapeutic relationship cannot be overemphasized as it is a factor that transcends therapeutic techniques and is related to therapeutic efficacy and effectiveness (Roberts & Yeager, 2006). Regardless of the amount of techniques, clinical experience, and training a practitioner has, if the therapeutic relationship has not been established, potential therapeutic gains will likely be diminished. As with any treatment approach, use of these interventions should occur within the confines of a solid alliance between the client and therapist. By establishing a warm, accepting environment and using cognitively and developmentally appropriate tools, even the most difficult and challenging clients may feel safe and trusting enough to engage in the therapeutic process. Play-based interventions help create this type of environment and lay the foundation for the rapport necessary for a strong therapeutic alliance to emerge and flourish. This relationship becomes the core from which the tools contained in this manual will be most effective.

Theoretical Orientation

The foundation for the interventions contained in this manual comes from clinical theory and clinically sound practice principles. Several of the interventions are grounded in cognitive-behavioral theory and many techniques incorporate elements of behavioral rehearsal or transitional objects to assist with the process of generalizing skills to settings beyond the therapeutic milieu.

When employing these interventions, practitioners must remain grounded in clinical theory, practice principles, and play therapy theory. These techniques are not to be employed indiscriminately, but are intended to be matched to the child's treatment needs using a prescriptive approach. A prescriptive approach involves creating a comprehensive treatment plan based on a variety of therapeutic constructs whereby play interventions are selected to alleviate symptoms and problems and achieve specific treatment goals (Schaefer, 2001). In this way, interventions are prescriptively selected to fit the treatment needs of the child. Each chapter contains different ways to address therapeutic areas and provides practitioners with a selection of interventions from which to choose. Interventions are intended to serve as clinical tools and are meant to be incorporated into a solid clinical framework. They are not intended to create a "cookie-cutter" approach to therapy, nor are they intended to stand on their own.

Clinical Judgment

Even when using manualized tightly controlled treatments, good clinical judgment is imperative when utilizing psychotherapy techniques with children. Many factors need to be considered when working with children, adolescents, and families including individual clinical needs, the client's personality and interests, the current and past diagnosis, treatment goals, and the stage of treatment. With the ever-growing literature on evidence-based treatment approaches for specific diagnoses and conditions, practitioners are compelled to use their clinical judgment to explore these protocols, as well as other standard-of-care approaches when working with their clients. Practitioners are also responsible for considering contra indicators for using the activities contained in this manual, such as not introducing the interventions that address sexual abuse prior to establishing a therapeutic relationship and assessing the client's repertoire of coping strategies. In addition, the style of the therapist also needs to be considered. Even for well-grounded techniques, if components of the intervention do not fit for the clinician or the clinician is uncomfortable utilizing the technique, the therapeutic benefits may be lost or diminished. In that regard, these interventions can be modified by the therapist as needed. For example, eliminating a portion of a technique or combining elements of one technique with elements of another are clinical modifications that can be made if necessary to make the intervention fit for different clinical styles.

Cultural Competency

Cultural considerations are an essential component of all mental health practice. Interventions must be implemented in a culturally sensitive and competent manner. Since culture is more than just ethnicity, culture should be defined in a broad manner and multiple areas of diversity should be considered when implementing these techniques. Areas of diversity include, but are not limited to, such things as socioeconomic status, religion, sexual orientation, child-rearing customs, and family structure/composition. Knowing the symbols, meanings, and messages of these cultural influences will assist play therapists in utilizing the techniques and interventions included in this book in a culturally competent manner. Reading and studying about these different areas of cultural diversity provides another avenue to become more culturally sensitive and aware. However, since it is impossible to be proficient and fully knowledgeable about every area of cultural diversity, it is important to ask the client and their family about their cultural beliefs and influences.

Clinical Training and Supervision

Play therapy training is essential for any practitioner utilizing this manual. As with any area of clinical practice, on-going training and supervision are important components of clinical practice and professional growth. Professionals working with children, adolescents, and families are strongly encouraged to obtain continuing education specific to play therapy and seek professional associations specializing in therapeutic work in this area. As a means to this end, professional organizations are listed at the end of this book. The techniques contained in this manual do not make an individual a play therapist. Continued training and professional development is of paramount importance and is the responsibility of each individual practitioner.

Likewise, general clinical training and supervision are necessary for practitioners using the interventions in this manual. The techniques included in this book are intended to supplement clinical practice as the practitioner remains theoretically grounded. Emphasis should be placed on utilizing these interventions to obtain therapeutic gains and address treatment goals. Both clinical and play therapy supervision will assist in this process.

Generalization of Therapeutic Skills

In treatment, generalization of skills to settings beyond the therapeutic milieu is one of the most important, but often overlooked, parts of therapy. Behavioral rehearsal, in which target behaviors and skills are practiced with feedback provided, and transitional objects, which serve to remind the client of the therapeutic concepts acquired in the session, may serve to facilitate this process, and subsequently are components of many of the techniques in this book. In addition to assisting with generalization, transitional objects may provide caregivers with a concrete representation of what was addressed during the session and can help parents understand that play therapy is not "just play." It is essential for clients to practice and rehearse skills learned during sessions in order for them to use these skills in their natural settings outside of the therapy session.

Traumatized Clients

Traumatized children and adolescents are frequently encountered in the mental health field and present unique challenges for practitioners. Special care must be utilized when working with this population and applying the interventions contained in this manual. Specifically, it is imperative that therapists first assess the traumatized individual's repertoire of coping strategies, assess for ongoing danger, and ensure basic safety issues are addressed prior to employing the activities in this manual. Practitioners who do not address these areas in advance may create iatrogenic effects in which the intervention may be counterproductive and potentially harmful.

Incorporating Parents/Caregivers

Involving caregivers and/or the entire family system in treatment may serve to assist in the generalization process and can often be crucial to the success of treatment. If clinically indicated, the caregiver and other relevant family members should be active participants in the therapeutic process. The caregiver should be included at the end of each session for the child to explain the technique utilized during the session and to show the caregiver what skills the child learned. Older children can "teach" their caregivers the skills learned at the end of the session and the therapist can enlist the caregiver to "coach" the child to practice the newly learned skills. The therapist can use this opportunity to explain how the skills relate to the child's treatment goals. In addition, the therapist should encourage the caregiver and other appropriate family members to model and reinforce the therapeutic skills as well as praise the child for using the skills in between sessions. The therapist is also encouraged to educate the caregiver and other relevant family members on the use of play therapy and the therapeutic rationale for employing this approach with children and adolescents. Practitioners must also consider that certain disorders might best be treated by focusing on the parent-child relationship or increasing parenting skills.

Family Play Therapy

Although an individual child or adolescent may be the identified client, working with the entire family system can be an equally important part of therapy. Family play therapy combines family therapy and play therapy to involve participation of the entire family system in order to gain an understanding of family functioning, communication patterns, dynamics, interactions, and relationships (Gil, 2006). There are many benefits of family play therapy including decreasing resistance, promoting enjoyment, and facilitating family relatedness (Gil, 2007). The interventions contained in this manual can be utilized in family play therapy to not only gain an understanding of the aforementioned areas, but also to provide the family with the opportunity to learn and acquire the therapeutic skills emphasized via the technique. When utilized in family play therapy, these techniques provide the clinician information relating to the process of how the family approaches tasks as well as the content pertaining to the therapeutic skills emphasized in the intervention.

Purposeful Use of Self

The therapist's participation in the interventions is another avenue that provides the opportunity for the modeling of therapeutic skills. For techniques utilized in individual therapy, the therapist provides the second player for the interventions. This provides an opportunity to join with the child, strengthen the therapeutic alliance, and model the skills emphasized in the technique. The more playful and engaging the therapist is during the interventions, the more relaxed the child may become, the lower the child's defenses may be, and the more sharing and growth the child may experience. However, clinicians should be prepared to respond to potentially awkward questions from the child and monitor self-disclosure to ensure disclosure is used sparingly and only when clinically relevant and appropriate.

Preparation and Use

The materials selected for techniques are intended to be engaging and creative but also readily available and inexpensive. Clinicians are encouraged to modify or substitute materials as necessary to fit interventions to the clinical setting, style, and population the techniques will be utilized for. Techniques vary in regard to how much preparation is required prior to use.

Cautionary Reminder

As a cautionary reminder, great care must be utilized by practitioners incorporating these play-based activities into their work to ensure the activities are employed in a clinically sound manner and are not haphazardly applied. The techniques contained in this manual do not comprise a complete treatment program, but may provide additional clinical support and intervention to supplement a client's comprehensive treatment plan. Interventions are to be utilized in a thoughtful, purposeful manner to alleviative symptoms, address treatment goals, and assist in improving clients' overall functioning.

Chapter 1: Assessment & Engagement

The assessment and engagement process is essential as it establishes the therapeutic connection from which growth and change will occur. Interventions in this chapter focus on engaging and connecting with clients in a developmentally appropriate way to assist in collecting assessment information. Because many children, adolescents, and families enter treatment involuntarily, normalizing the process of therapy and highlighting the importance of addressing presenting problems as opposed to ignoring or "forgetting" them is a crucial concept for the early stages of treatment. The creative approach of these assessment and engagement interventions will serve to assist in this process.

During the assessment process, it is not only necessary to gather information from parents and collateral sources, but also from the child. This is particularly important as some clinical literature indicates parents may underreport children's internalizing symptoms when the parent's report of the symptoms is compared to the child's report. To address this, interventions in this chapter offer tools for collecting information from the child's perspective to help clarify treatment goals.

Generally, assessment and engagement techniques are employed in the early stages of treatment to gather information and assist with the process of treatment planning. However, because assessment is an on-going process, the interventions presented in this chapter can be utilized at any point in therapy to serve as a gauge to measure and monitor therapeutic gains and progress.

Interventions utilized during the assessment and engagement portion of therapy often set the stage for treatment. Therefore, the creative and engaging nature of the interventions included in this chapter will help provide a therapeutic tone that communicates treatment is manageable, interesting, and fun.

Ice Breaker

Intervention Summary

This getting-to-know-you activity is a modified version of the board game Don't Break the Ice™ (Milton Bradley). Colored stickers are placed on the underside of the game ice cubes with each color corresponding to one of six categories (likes, dislikes, self/family/friends, hopes/dreams, ask a question to the other player, treat). As players knock ice cubes out of the game, they share something about themselves based on the color of the sticker located on the underside of the ice cube.

Purpose

- Engagement
- Begin to establish the therapeutic relationship
- Acquaint the client and therapist

Modality

- Individual
- Group
- Family

Age Range

- 5–18 years

Materials

- Don't Break the Ice™ (Milton Bradley)
- Star stickers
- Small candy/stickers (optional)

Description

Engagement begins at the first contact and is essential to establish the therapeutic relationship. This technique is intended to "break the ice" between the client and therapist and provides an engaging way for individuals to get acquainted.

The game Don't Break the Ice™ (Milton Bradley) is played using the regular rules of play and the additional rule that after players have tapped an ice cube out of the game, they share something about themselves according to the color of the star sticker located on the underside of the ice cube.

Prior to the game, colored star stickers are placed on the underside of each ice cube. A traditional package of self-adhesive foil star stickers, which can be purchased at discount stores, craft stores, or online, contains five colors (i.e. blue, red, green, gold, and silver). For this intervention, an additional "smiley face" category is created by drawing a smiley face on one color resulting in six categories of stickers (i.e. blue, red, green, gold, silver, and smiley face). Since there are 36 cubes in the game, six stickers of each color/category will be used. Each sticker color corresponds to a different category. Categories include the following:

- ◆ Blue = Something I like
- ◆ Red = Something I don't like
- ◆ Green = Something about myself, my family, or my friends
- ◆ Gold = One of my hopes or dreams
- ◆ Silver = Ask a question to the other player
- ◆ Smiley Face = Free Choice & Treat/Sticker (optional)

Note: The Don't Break the Ice™ (Milton Bradley) game has one large ice cube that is the size of four individual ice cubes. When the game is played using the traditional rules, this large ice cube serves to hold the ice skater. In addition to the large ice cube, the game typically comes with extra small ice cubes that serve as replacement ice cubes in the event that pieces of the game become lost or misplaced. For this therapeutic version of the game, the replacement ice cubes are used in lieu of the large ice cube. If there is not enough extra ice cubes to fill the frame of the game, the large ice cube can be used and four star stickers can be placed on the underside. If the large ice cube is used, a player who knocks this ice cube out must respond to all four categories according to the star stickers located on the underside of the cube.

The game Don't Break the Ice™ (Milton Bradley) is played using the regular rules of play plus the additional rule that after each player's turn, the player must share about themselves based on the categories assigned to the stickers on the bottom of each ice cube that fell during their turn. If an ice cube includes a star sticker with a smiley face, the player selects a piece of candy and responds to a category of their choice. Stickers can be used instead of candy if desired. The use of candy or stickers is an optional part of the intervention, but the prospect of "winning" something during the course of the activity may lower defenses and incorporates an additional component of engagement and playfulness to the technique.

Throughout the activity, players get better acquainted by sharing non-threatening information in an engaging, yet structured manner. Using this intervention in the early stage of treatment assists in creating a playful, client-friendly therapeutic environment and orienting the client to the process of play therapy.

All Tied Up

Intervention Summary

The importance of addressing and processing abusive and traumatic events as opposed to ignoring them is communicated by tying up a co-therapist or an adult family member in yarn labeled with symptoms of trauma as depicted in the therapeutic story *"Brave Bart: A Story for Traumatized and Grieving Children"* (Sheppard, 1998). Until these symptoms are explored and addressed, the individual remains "all tied up" with the problems.

Purpose

- Engagement
- Explore the process and benefits of therapy
- Demonstrate the importance of dealing with traumatic/abusive events
- Reduce the element of secrecy inherent in traumatic/abusive events
- Normalize common reactions and responses to trauma/abuse
- Assess symptoms and problems impacting the client
- Identify coping skills to address the residual affects of trauma/abuse

Modality

- Group
- Family

Age Range

- 7–12 years

Materials

- Therapeutic story *"Brave Bart: A Story for Traumatized and Grieving Children"* (Sheppard, 1998)
- Adult/group co-facilitator or large puppet
- Thick yarn

- Marker
- Masking tape
- Scissors

(NOTE: This intervention is intended to be utilized in a group setting when there are two group facilitators or in a family session with a protective, supportive adult. The description below is written for use in a group setting. If the therapist has concerns that "tying" a person up with the symptoms related to trauma might trigger a trauma response from the client, a large puppet can be used instead.)

Description

Many victims of trauma and abuse enter treatment with avoidance of their traumatic experience, including discussion or play related to it. This intervention focuses on normalizing the residual impact of traumatic and abusive experiences and providing a visual representation of the importance of processing and addressing this material.

Following a discussion regarding the importance of talking about abusive and traumatic events despite our tendency to avoid these things, the therapist reads the story "*Brave Bart*." In the story, a cat named Bart experiences an unidentified trauma described as "a bad, sad, and scary thing," and afterward, begins to experience various post-traumatic symptoms (i.e. nightmares, bouts of crying, anxiety, withdrawal, etc.). Eventually, Bart receives help from "Helping Hannah," an adult cat who metaphorically represents a therapist, and the posttraumatic symptoms begin to dissipate.

After reading the story, group members identify and discuss symptoms Bart experienced as a result of the "bad, sad, and scary thing." The symptoms depicted in the story of "*Brave Bart*" serve as a foundation for normalizing potential problems the clients may be experiencing. For each symptom that is identified, a piece of thick yarn is tied around one of the group facilitators. Each piece of yarn is labeled with the corresponding symptom using masking tape. For example, if the symptom "being scared" is identified, a piece of yarn is tied around the therapist and labeled as "scared."

By the time group members have identified Bart's various symptoms, the facilitator will be "all tied up" with the symptoms associated with the "bad, sad, and scary thing." A discussion ensues regarding the fact that the facilitator cannot function in life and complete daily activities while being "all tied up." To emphasize this, group members instruct the facilitator to enact day-to-day activities such as brushing their teeth, walking up a flight of stairs, or raising their arms above their head. Since the facilitator is "all tied up" with unresolved issues secondary to trauma and abuse, the facilitator will have limited success in completing these activities.

After group members reach the conclusion that the facilitator cannot function unless the facilitator is untied and "released" from the symptoms, coping skills to mediate the identified symptoms are discussed. As members identify potential coping strategies for each symptom, they are allowed to cut the piece of yarn that represents the symptom being discussed. By the end of the intervention, all of the pieces of yarn will have been cut and the facilitator will no longer be "all tied up."

The metaphor of being "all tied up" serves to engage group members in a discussion to facilitate an understanding of the importance of processing and addressing their history of trauma and abuse. As part of this discussion, becoming "all tied up" if thoughts, feelings, and symptoms related to the trauma or abuse are avoided, minimized, or denied is explored in a manner that connects the therapeutic concept to the clients' own lives and histories.

This activity provides a developmentally appropriate way to highlight the importance of addressing traumatic material. However, contra indicators for using this intervention include children and families that are still in crisis or danger, dissociative children, or children who have a co-morbid psychotic disorder. Similarly, this intervention is intended to provide a general understanding of the importance of dealing with traumatic or abusive material and is not intended to process the client's specific history of trauma or abuse as the client will likely not possess the coping skills necessary to manage emotions and reactions that may surface as the traumatic event is processed during the early stages of treatment.

How Big is the Problem?

Intervention Summary

Children's report of their internalizing symptoms and distress may be more accurate than reports provided by others. This assessment technique gives children the opportunity to indicate whether or not a particular symptom is a problem for them and to what extent. Children accomplish this by placing rice, macaroni noodles, beads or other types of small media onto index cards with various internalizing symptoms written on them. Children's placement of more rice, noodles, or beads on the symptom card represents the child's perception of a larger problem.

Purpose

- Assess areas of distress and difficulty from the child's perspective
- Assess internalizing symptoms
- Normalize the existence of presenting problems
- Provide the child with the opportunity to quantify problem areas
- Engagement
- Empowerment
- Validate the child's perceptions

Modality

- Individual

Age Range

- 7–14 years

Materials

- Index cards with various symptoms and problems written on them (see attached)
- Rice, macaroni noodles, beads or other small media

Description

Internalizing distress and symptoms, which include things not easily observable such as depression, anxiety, preoccupation, intrusive recollections, and avoidance, may be best reported by the child (Deblinger & Heflin, 1996; Rev, Schrader, & Morris-Yates, 1992). This technique provides the child with the opportunity to quantify his or her problems and symptoms to provide the therapist with a more accurate clinical picture.

Prior to the session, the therapist writes various problems and symptoms the child may be experiencing on index cards. The symptoms and problems selected should match the client's diagnosis and case conceptualization. For example, symptoms selected for a child conceptualized as suffering from Posttraumatic Stress Disorder would include clinical indicators of avoidance and intrusive recollections. Each index card should have one problem written on it. Particular attention should be given to internalizing symptoms such as sadness, anxiety, guilt, preoccupation, and low self-esteem. During the course of the intervention, the rice, noodles, or beads are utilized by the child to identify the child's problems. For problems the child identifies as significant, the amount of rice, noodles, or beads used will signify how big the problem is.

Although the emphasis of this intervention is on assessing internalizing difficulties, externalizing difficulties can be included as well. This provides the child with the opportunity to quantify a variety of problem areas and communicates to the child that his or her opinion is important in the therapeutic process. In addition, the child's report of his or her externalizing symptoms, when compared to the reports of others such as parents or teachers, may serve as a guide for determining whether the child is accurately describing his or her perceptions or minimizing symptoms to avoid being seen negatively by the therapist.

At the beginning of the session, the therapist explains to the child that although lots of people in the child's life may have thoughts or ideas about what is bothering the child, it is the child who knows what is *really* bothering them. During this activity, the child gets to be the expert by identifying his or her own problems and difficulties. The therapist explains each index card has a different problem written on it. The therapist will read each card and place the card on the table. The child will decide whether or not the problem on the card is an area of difficulty for him or her and will use the rice to show how big the problem is. The bigger the problem, the more rice the child will place on the index card.

The therapist should provide a visual example for the child. For instance, the therapist can demonstrate by stating, "I will show you an example. If *'I feel worried'* is the problem on the card and feeling worried is not a problem for you, then you won't put any rice on the card. However, if feeling worried is a small problem for you, you'll place a small amount of rice on the card. If feeling worried is a medium problem for you, you'll place a medium amount of rice on the card, and if it is a *big* problem, you'll put a large amount of rice on the card."

To ensure the therapist has a clear understanding of the child's perspective, clarifying questions should be asked during the initial stages of the intervention to clarify whether the amount of rice placed on a card indicates a small, medium, or large problem. For example, the therapist can ask, "Based on the amount of rice you placed on this card, it looks as though this is a medium problem for you. Is that right?" Clarifying questions serve to assist the therapist in understanding the meaning of the amount of rice used by the child.

This intervention allows the therapist to gather assessment information from the child's perspective and highlights internalizing symptoms the parent or caregiver may be either unaware of or not attuned to. This technique often reveals influential, yet previously underreported difficulties. As the intervention progresses, identified problems can be normalized for the child.

A list of possible internalizing and externalizing symptoms is provided on the following pages to serve as a guide for this technique. The therapist should utilize clinical judgment when selecting symptoms as not all of the problems listed will apply to all children. If a problem area does not apply, the therapist should not select that problem for the game. In addition to the symptoms listed, there should be an "other" category in case a symptom is overlooked or missed.

This intervention creates a non-threatening way to explore the child's perception of the presenting problem while creating distance and safety. Not only does this intervention engage the child, but it also facilitates the development of the therapeutic relationship by communicating to the child that his or her input is essential in the therapeutic process. The technique also gives children the opportunity to express their thoughts regarding problem areas and allows identification of discrete properties of a problem to help identify specific as opposed to global distress.

Since assessment is an on-going process, this intervention can be repeated and utilized throughout the course of treatment to informally assess progress in the area of reducing internalizing symptoms. It is also important to note that some children underreport problems and symptoms to protect their parents. Subsequently, it may be best to complete this activity without the caregiver present.

Internalizing Symptoms

- I feel scared.
- I feel worried.
- I feel sad.
- I have bad dreams.
- I have trouble sleeping.
- I don't have many friends.
- I can't stop thinking about my problems.
- School is hard for me.
- I have a secret that really bothers me.
- I have been hurt by someone.
- I am sick a lot.
- Bad things that have happened pop into my head.
- It's hard for me to talk about my feelings and problems.
- I feel like a bad kid.
- It's hard for me to pay attention.
- I feel like things will never get better.
- I think about hurting myself on purpose.
- I don't really like myself.
- I feel like no one cares about me.
- There are lots of problems in my family.
- I try to forget about my problems to make them go away.

Externalizing Symptoms

- I hit people.
- I break or throw things.
- It's hard for me to sit still.
- It's hard for me to keep my hands and feet to myself.

- I touch kids in ways I'm not supposed to.
- I don't follow the rules.
- I don't listen to grown-ups.
- I tell lies.
- I take or steal things.
- I lose my temper easily.
- I throw temper tantrums.
- I yell and scream.
- I say bad words.
- I get teased.
- I wet the bed.

Weighing Things Out

Intervention Summary

To assess the child's repertoire of coping skills, a balancing scale is utilized to provide a visual representation of the child's coping strategies. Adaptive and maladaptive behaviors and strategies are written on index cards. The client places a decorative marble or other type of weight on the corresponding side of the scale if they engage in the strategy. When the technique is complete, there is a visual representation of the child's repertoire of coping strategies. This provides the therapist with assessment information to determine whether the child has enough adaptive coping strategies to move into the working phase of treatment.

Purpose

- Assess the child's repertoire of coping strategies
- Assist the child in differentiating between adaptive and maladaptive coping strategies
- Reinforce the use of adaptive coping strategies
- Determine if a child has enough adaptive coping strategies to move into the working phase of treatment

Modality

- Individual

Age Range

- 7–12 years

Materials

- Balancing Bear Scale™ (purchased from Discount School Supply)
- Index cards
- Marker
- Decorative marbles or another media that can serve as a weight (i.e. small polished stones, etc.)

Preparation

Before the session, the therapist writes different adaptive and maladaptive coping strategies on index cards. Strategies selected should be based upon the child's age and clinical profile. There should be an equal number of adaptive and maladaptive strategies identified. A list of possible strategies is provided on the following page to serve as a guide. Blank index cards should be available for the child to write adaptive and maladaptive strategies as needed.

Description

Prior to delving into traumatic issues or emotionally-laden presenting problems, practitioners must ascertain whether the client has an adequate repertoire of coping strategies to manage the emotions and distress that may arise during the working phase of treatment. This assessment intervention helps the child differentiate between positive, adaptive, helpful coping strategies versus negative, maladaptive, unhelpful strategies. In addition, the technique allows the therapist to assess whether the child is currently utilizing more adaptive strategies or more maladaptive strategies. If the child is utilizing more maladaptive strategies, treatment should focus on expanding the child's repertoire of adaptive coping skills prior to moving into the working phase of treatment where traumatic material or emotionally-laden issues will be explored.

At the beginning of the session, the therapist explains to the child that everyone responds to problems differently. Sometimes when we are trying to handle a problem, we do things that make the situation better and sometimes we do things that make it worse. This activity will allow the child and therapist to explore this area.

The technique is divided into two parts. During the first part, the child will decide whether the strategy written on the card would make a situation better or worse. If the strategy would make a situation better, the card is put on the table in front of one side of the scale and if it would make the situation worse, the card is placed on the table in front of the other side of the scale. After the child decides which side of the scale to put the card in front of, a decorative marble or weight (i.e. small stone, etc.) is placed on the index card. This marble/weight is utilized during the second part of the activity. During the first portion of the activity, the focus is for the child to differentiate between positive and negative coping strategies.

During the next part of the activity, each strategy is reviewed and the child indicates whether or not he or she uses the skill by placing the decorative marble or weight on the card onto the corresponding side of the scale. Once the skills have been reviewed and the marbles are placed on the scale, there is a visual representation of whether the child is using more adaptive coping strategies (i.e. helpful strategies) or more maladaptive strategies (i.e. unhelpful strategies). This visual representation is processed with the child with an emphasis on discussing the strategies the child possesses and the implications this has on the next step in treatment. The use of maladaptive or "unhelpful" strategies should be normalized to avoid the child feeling ashamed or judged as a result of engaging in maladaptive strategies.

This intervention provides the therapist with an assessment of the child's repertoire of coping strategies and information as to whether or not the child has enough adaptive coping strategies to enter the working phase of treatment. If the child does not have enough adaptive strategies, treatment should focus on interventions that emphasize developing and strengthening adaptive coping skills.

Positive/Helpful Strategies

- Sports
- Music
- Playing
- Talking to someone I trust
- Drawing/Coloring
- Exercising
- TV/Movie
- Video Game

Negative/Unhelpful Strategies

- Hitting
- Yelling
- Running Away
- Swearing
- Thinking about things that make me feel worse
- Hurting myself on purpose
- Pretending everything is fine when I really feel upset

Chapter 2: Emotional Expression

Regardless of the identified presenting problem or diagnosis, assisting children, adolescents, and families in identifying and processing their emotions is a cornerstone of treatment. Whether emotional difficulties are primary issues, as in the case of depression or anxiety, or secondary issues, as in the case of divorce or social rejection, a person's ability to effectively communicate feelings in a supportive environment is essential to healthy emotional well-being.

There are several factors that result in people experiencing difficulty expressing their feelings. These factors include such things as possessing a limited emotional vocabulary, internalizing or avoiding feelings, or believing one's feelings are "weird" or abnormal. Abusive events, traumatic events and other psychosocial stressors create further complications to healthy emotional expression.

The techniques presented in this chapter utilize creative materials in conjunction with a play-based approach to lower defenses, provide distancing, and create a safe, engaging format from which various feelings and emotions can be identified and processed. It is hoped that these interventions may reduce emotional distress, diminish internalization, and decrease acting-out behaviors.

Revealing Your Feelings

Intervention Summary

Since many clients avoid discussing distressing emotions, this technique was developed to facilitate emotional expression of "hidden" feelings. The therapist uses the "invisible" marker from the package of Crayola Color Changeable Markers™ to write various feelings inside shapes (i.e. squares, circles, triangles, etc.). Players take turns coloring a shape with one of the Color Changeable Markers™, revealing the feeling word written inside the shape. Each feeling is processed.

Purpose

- Facilitate emotional expression
- Validate and normalize emotions
- Broaden the client's emotional vocabulary
- Identify coping strategies

Modality

- Individual
- Group
- Family

Age Range

- 5–18 years

Materials

- Paper
- Black marker
- Crayola Color Changeable Markers™
- Small candy (Jolly Ranchers™, Hershey Kisses™, etc.) or stickers (optional)

Description

Prior to the session, the therapist draws various shapes (i.e. squares, circles, triangles, hearts, etc.) on the paper using a black marker. The shapes need to be large enough for feeling words to be written inside. The therapist writes various feeling words or the word "Treat" (optional) inside the shapes using the invisible marker from the package of Crayola Color Changeable Markers™.

During the session, players take turns coloring a shape with one of the Color Changeable Markers™. Coloring the shape will reveal the feeling previously written inside the shape with the invisible marker. After the feeling has been revealed, the player discusses a time he or she experienced that emotion. If the word "Treat" is revealed, the player selects a piece of candy and discusses a feeling of their choice. Stickers can be used instead of candy, if desired. The use of candy or stickers is an optional part of the intervention, but the prospect of "winning" something during the course of the activity may lower defenses and incorporates an additional component of playfulness to the technique.

Throughout the activity, the therapist has the opportunity to normalize and validate the emotions discussed by the client. As an additional component, coping skills to manage emotional distress can be identified and discussed.

This technique allows the therapist to select specific emotions pertaining to the client's diagnosis, treatment plan, or treatment goals. For example, if the client is experiencing depression, the therapist can select "depressed," "sad," and "upset" as three of the feelings to write inside the shapes. For an anxious child, the words "anxious," "nervous," and "worried" can be selected. The ability to prescriptively select specific emotions allows clinical discretion to ensure treatment goals are addressed.

Feelings Connect Four

Intervention Summary

The checkers in the Connect Four® (Hasbro) game are labeled with various emotions or the word "Treat" (optional). The board game Connect Four® is played using the regular rules of play and the additional rule that when players successfully achieve a Connect Four, they must talk about a time they experienced the feelings written on the checkers in their line.

Purpose

- Facilitate emotional expression
- Validate and normalize emotions
- Develop and expand the client's emotional vocabulary
- Identify coping strategies

Modality

- Individual
- Family

Age Range

- 7–18 years

Materials

- Connect Four® (Hasbro)
- Label maker or strips of paper
- Small candy (Jolly Ranchers™, Hershey Kisses™, etc.) or stickers (optional)

Description

This intervention is a modified version of the Milton Bradley board game Connect Four®. Prior to the session, the therapist uses a label maker to label each checker in the Connect Four® game with a feeling word. Several of the checkers can also be labeled with the word "Treat" (optional). If a label maker is not available, the therapist can write various feelings on strips of paper and place the strips in a bowl.

The game Connect Four® (Hasbro) is played using the regular rules of play and the additional rule that in order to win the game, the player who achieves a "connect four" must talk about a time they experienced the feelings on the checkers in their "connect four" line. If the "connect four" line includes a checker labeled "Treat," the player selects a piece of candy and discusses a feeling of their choice. Stickers can be used instead of candy, if desired. The use of candy or stickers is an optional part of the intervention, but the prospect of "winning" something during the course of the activity may lower defenses and incorporates an additional component of playfulness to the technique.

If checkers are not individually labeled but strips of paper with feeling words are used instead, a player who achieves a "connect four" selects four strips of paper from the bowl and processes a time they experienced the feelings written on the paper. If the word "Treat" is selected, the player selects a piece of candy and discusses a feeling of their choice.

Throughout the activity, the therapist has the opportunity to normalize and validate the emotions discussed by the client. As an additional component, coping skills to manage emotional distress can be identified and discussed.

This technique allows the therapist to select specific emotions pertaining to the client's diagnosis, treatment plan, or treatment goals. For example, if the client is experiencing depression, the therapist can select "depressed," "sad," and "upset" as three emotions to label the game pieces with. For an anxious child, the feelings "anxious," "nervous," and "worried" can be selected. The ability to prescriptively select specific emotions allows clinical discretion to ensure treatment goals are addressed.

Feelings Hide-and-Seek

Intervention Summary

This technique is a therapeutic version of the childhood game hide-and-seek in which feelings are initially hidden, and through the course of hide-and-seek are found and discussed. Feelings are written on index cards that are hidden at varying levels of difficulty around the room. Players take turns finding the hidden feeling cards and processing a time they experienced the emotion written on the card.

Purpose

- Facilitate emotional expression
- Validate and normalize emotions
- Develop and expand the client's emotional vocabulary
- Identify coping strategies

Modality

- Individual
- Group
- Family

Age Range

- 5–18 years

Materials

- Index cards with various feelings written on them
- Tape
- Small candy (Jolly Ranchers™, Hershey Kisses™, etc.) or stickers (optional)

Description

This technique is a therapeutic version of the popular childhood game hide-and-seek. However, instead of people hiding, the therapist has hidden cards with various feeling words.

Prior to the session, the therapist writes various feelings on index cards. For durability, cards can be printed on card stock and laminated. If desired, the word "Treat," "Sticker," or a smiley face can be written on several of the cards. During the course of play, if a player finds one of these cards, they select a treat, sticker, or other small prize and discuss a feeling of their choice. Although this is an optional element, the prospect of "winning" something during the course of the activity may lower defenses and incorporates an additional component of playfulness to the technique.

Using tape, the index cards are hidden around the room at varying levels of difficulty. For younger children, the cards will be hidden in obvious places and for older, more sophisticated children and adolescents, the cards can be hidden more secretively.

The therapist explains that in many situations, people ignore their feelings and keep them hidden instead of dealing with them. Even though this may seem effective, "hidden" feelings still exist and continue to bother the person until the feelings are brought out into the open and addressed.

In this game, feelings start out hidden and through the course of hide-and-seek, are found and discussed. During the intervention, players take turns finding the hidden feeling cards and processing a time they experienced the feeling written on the card. If this technique is used in individual therapy, the therapist plays the game with the client. If it is utilized in group or family therapy, the therapist has the option of playing along or serving as a facilitator.

As feelings are chosen for the intervention, the therapist should prescriptively match the emotions to the client's presenting problem, diagnosis, and treatment goals. For example, if a child suffers from a form of depression, emotions selected could include feelings such as sad, depressed, and upset. If a child's therapeutic needs focus more on the anxiety continuum, emotions selected could include anxious, nervous, and worried.

During the activity, the therapist has the opportunity to normalize and validate the child's emotions. As an additional component, coping skills to manage emotional distress can be identified and discussed.

Chapter 3: Coping Skills

In conjunction with being able to appropriately identify and express feelings, it is equally important that children, adolescents, and families are able to cope with and manage emotional distress. This chapter focuses on providing strategies to manage emotions in effective, productive ways. For younger children, interventions in this chapter emphasize active coping strategies that focus on practical strategies a child can utilize to reduce emotional reactivity. For older, more cognitively mature children, adolescents, and adults, techniques focus on the development of cognitive coping strategies that emphasize identifying and altering maladaptive thought patterns and replacing these patterns with more adaptive patterns.

To assist in the process of generalization, some interventions in this chapter incorporate behavioral rehearsal in which target behaviors and skills are practiced and the clinician provides feedback to the child regarding the acquired skills. Transitional objects, which serve to remind the client of the therapeutic concept acquired in the session, are incorporated into some of the techniques as well. When clinically indicated and appropriate, involving parents and caregivers in the treatment process may provide additional support for generalizing the coping skills learned through these techniques to settings beyond the therapeutic milieu.

Techniques presented in this chapter are utilized in treatment to assist children, adolescents, and families in expanding their repertoire of adaptive coping strategies in an effort to reduce both internalizing and externalizing problems and symptoms. In addition, these interventions can serve to empower clients to adaptively manage their emotions in a manner that facilitates their ability to confront and address problems and stressors more effectively.

Bubble Wrap

Intervention Summary

This developmentally appropriate technique uses construction paper and bubble packaging wrap to provide a concrete representation of coping strategies to manage emotional distress. The client selects squares of construction paper to quantify their level of emotional distress. For each square of construction paper, the client identifies one adaptive coping strategy to manage the distressing emotion. The construction paper is taped onto the bubble wrap and the bubbles are popped to signify that the emotional distress can be reduced by using the coping strategy.

Purpose

- Develop coping skills
- Facilitate emotional expression

Modality

- Individual
- Group
- Family

Age Range

- 6–12 years

Materials

- Bubble packaging wrap with extra large bubbles (cut into squares)
- Various colors of construction paper (cut into squares)
- Markers
- Tape

Description

This technique uses the desire to pop packaging wrap as a non-threatening medium to encourage children to identify coping skills to manage emotional distress. For this activity, the air in the bubble wrap symbolizes the feeling being targeted and popping the bubbles represents how coping strategies can reduce distressing emotions. Just as the child can conquer the bubbles, he or she can overcome emotional distress.

Prior to the session, the therapist cuts the bubble wrap and colored construction paper into squares. At the onset of the session, the therapist and child discuss the fact that some feelings, such as happy and excited, are easy feelings to experience whereas other emotions, such as scared, sad, or worried, are difficult to manage.

The child is encouraged to identify one feeling he or she experiences that is particularly difficult. If clinically indicated, the therapist can lead this discussion to facilitate identification of a feeling that is consistent with the child's diagnosis or treatment goals. The child selects a color of construction paper to represent the identified emotion. For example, if the child has identified feeling "sad" as particularly difficult, blue construction paper may be selected to represent "sad." The child is instructed to select as many pieces of construction paper necessary to show how much of the feeling he or she experiences. The more squares of construction paper selected, the more distress the child experiences. Using the example above, if the child feels only a little sad, only a few squares of blue construction paper will be selected whereas if the child feels really sad, he or she will select a large number of squares.

After the construction paper has been selected, the child is instructed to identify one coping strategy for each square of construction paper selected. Using the example above, if the child selected ten squares of blue construction paper, he or she would identify ten adaptive coping skills to use when feeling sad. As each coping skill is identified, it is written or drawn on the square of construction paper. The construction paper is taped onto a square of bubble wrap and set aside. Since identifying a large number of adaptive coping strategies may be difficult for some clients, the clinician can create a list of strategies from which the client can choose from. This list should be tailored to fit the needs of each client.

After a coping skill is identified for each square of construction paper, the child selects one square at a time, says, "When I feel *(feeling word),* I can *(coping skill)*" (i.e. "When I feel **sad**, I can **talk to someone I trust**"), and proceeds to pop all the bubbles on the bubble packaging wrap. This is repeated for each piece of construction paper until all the bubble wrap is popped. Symbolically, this represents the coping skills overcoming and reducing the emotional distress.

To provide the child with the opportunity to utilize the identified coping skills, puppets can be employed to act out the coping skills. Both the therapist and child should take turns using the puppets to practice the coping skills. This gives the therapist the chance to model the skills as well as provide feedback to the child. This component of behavioral rehearsal may increase the likelihood that the child will utilize the skills in settings beyond the therapeutic environment.

As the coping skills are identified, the therapist writes the coping skills on a separate piece of paper. After the intervention is complete, the child can decorate the paper to create a poster of coping skills. The child can select three skills that he or she will try to use in between sessions. These coping skills can be denoted with a star, sticker, or other mark. The poster serves as a transitional object and a strategy to increase generalization of skills identified through the technique.

If clinically appropriate, the poster can be reviewed with the caregiver at the end of the session. The caregiver should be encouraged to reinforce and model the identified coping skills. This can be given as a specific homework assignment to facilitate generalization of the coping strategies to the child's natural environment.

Not only is the bubble wrap a fun, playful medium for the child, but the effort the child exerts to pop the bubbles provides a metaphor to explore the child's ability to master distressing emotions.

Balancing Out Your Feelings

Intervention Summary

The concept reflected in this technique is that one needs sufficient adaptive coping strategies to manage emotional distress. Clients begin the activity by quantifying their level of emotional distress. This distress is then offset by identifying a repertoire of adaptive strategies to cope with the distress. The client quantifies his or her level of emotional distress by placing weights into the "feeling" side of the scale. Players take turns "balancing out" this emotional distress by placing counterweights into the "coping" side of the scale with each counterweight representing a different adaptive coping strategy. Play continues until the "coping" side of the scale outweighs the "feeling" side of the scale.

Purpose

- Develop adaptive coping strategies
- Facilitate emotional expression

Modality

- Individual

Age Range

- 5–11 years

Materials

- Balancing Bear Scale™ (Discount School Supply)
- Decorative marbles or another type of media that can serve as a counter-weight (i.e. smooth stones, etc.)
- Paper and writing utensil
- Puppets (optional)

Description

The concept of coping skills is somewhat abstract and can be difficult for young children to grasp. When children are upset, adults frequently say something along the lines of, "You need to handle your feelings." However, this statement has more meaning for adolescents and adults than for young children given the cognitive development of children. Subsequently, this therapeutic activity is geared toward assisting children in developing an understanding of coping skills and arming the child with a repertoire of active coping strategies the child can utilize to reduce emotional distress.

The Balancing Bear Scale™ (Discount School Supply) is placed on the table with both sides of the scale in balance. The scale comes with different size plastic bears in primary colors of red, blue, and yellow. In this intervention, these bears will serve as "feeling bears" to provide a concrete representation of the emotion being focused on during this technique.

The "feeling bears" are placed on the table by one side of the scale. This side of the scale is the "feeling" side of the scale and will represent the amount of emotional distress the child experiences. The decorative marbles are placed on the table by the other side of the scale. This side of the scale is the "coping" side of the scale. Each marble will eventually be identified as a different coping strategy the child can employ when experiencing emotional distress.

At the onset of the session, the therapist and child identify the feeling that will be addressed during the activity. The therapist should lead this discussion to facilitate identification of a feeling that is consistent with the client's diagnosis and treatment goals. For example, if the child is an anxious child, feeling anxious, nervous, or worried can be targeted. The therapist and child engage in a discussion regarding feeling anxious and worried and identify various situations that evoke this emotion. The client is directed to use the "feeling bears" to show how anxious and worried they feel. The more "feeling bears" selected, the more anxious or worried the child feels. The child is instructed to place "feeling bears" into the "feeling" side of the scale to show how worried he or she feels. If the child feels a little bit worried, he or she might only place one to two "feeling bears" in the scale. However, if the child feels *really* worried, the child will put more "feeling bears" in the scale. In most situations, children use all, or nearly all, of the "feeling bears." The therapist utilizes this opportunity to normalize and validate the child's feelings.

Next, the therapist explains the concept of coping skills. A simple definition might be something like, "Coping skills are safe ways to handle feelings and include all the things you can do when you are worried to make yourself feel better. The more worry you have, the more coping skills you need. You need more than just one or two coping skills in case you try things that don't work."

The therapist tells the child that they are going to play a coping skills game with the scale. For the game, the marbles will represent coping skills such as riding a bike, talking to someone, getting a hug, or listening to music. During the game, players take turns placing a coping skill (i.e. decorative marble) into the coping side of the scale. Play continues until the "coping" side of the scale is heavier than the "feeling" side of the scale.

To provide the child with the opportunity to utilize the identified coping skills, puppets can be employed to act out the coping skills. Both the therapist and child should take turns using the puppets to practice the identified coping strategies. This gives the therapist the chance to model the skills as well as provide feedback to the child. This component of behavioral rehearsal may increase the likelihood the child will utilize the skills in settings beyond the therapeutic environment.

As the coping skills are identified, the therapist writes the coping skills on a piece of paper. After the intervention is complete, the child can decorate the paper to create a poster of coping skills. The child can select three skills that he or she will use in between sessions. These coping skills can be denoted with a star, sticker, or other mark. The poster serves as a transitional object and a strategy to increase generalization of skills identified through the technique.

If clinically appropriate, the coping skills poster can be reviewed with the caregiver at the end of the session. The caregiver should be encouraged to reinforce and model these coping strategies in between sessions as well.

This intervention presents a concrete representation of coping skills and provides a transitional object to assist with generalization of the therapeutic concepts. In addition, it allows the child the opportunity to quantify his or her feelings in a developmentally appropriate way and provides the therapist with a gauge of how much emotional distress the child is experiencing. This technique can be repeated during the course of treatment to monitor treatment progress.

Positive & Negative Thinking

Intervention Summary

Cognitive-behavioral therapy is grounded in the interdependence of cognitions, emotions, and behaviors with the basic premise of altering maladaptive beliefs and replacing these with more adaptive ones to invoke positive changes in the subsequent emotions and behaviors. This cognitive-behavioral intervention helps clients differentiate between adaptive and maladaptive cognitions and facilitates an understanding of the interplay between thoughts, feelings, and behaviors. Index cards with positive and negative cognitions are selected by players and read out loud using the tone of voice that reflects how each thought would typically make the person feel. The player indicates whether the statement is a positive thought or a negative thought and tapes the index card onto a page with either a happy face or a sad face to signify how the thought would make him or her feel.

Purpose

- Facilitate the development of positive thinking as a cognitive coping strategy
- Differentiate between positive and negative cognitions
- Replace maladaptive cognitions with more adaptive cognitions

Modality

- Individual
- Group
- Family

Age Range

- 8 years–Adults

Materials

- 8 ½ x 11 piece of paper or flip chart
- Marker
- Tape

- Index cards with general positive and negative thoughts (see attached)
- Small candy or stickers (optional)

Description

Cognitive-behavioral therapy (CBT), one of the most empirically supported treatment modalities, is grounded in the interdependence of cognitions, emotions, and behaviors with the basic premise that identifying and altering maladaptive beliefs and replacing these with more adaptive ones will invoke positive changes in subsequent feelings and behaviors. This technique is based upon CBT principles and focuses on assisting clients in understanding the interplay between thoughts, feelings, and behaviors and differentiating between general adaptive and maladaptive cognitions.

Prior to the session, the therapist writes general positive and negative thoughts on index cards. A list of possible positive and negative cognitions is listed on the following pages to serve as a guide. Each index card should have one statement written on it. If desired, the word "Treat," "Sticker," or a smiley face can be written on several cards. During the course of play, a player who selects one of these cards gets a treat, sticker, or other small prize. Although this is an optional part of the intervention, the prospect of "winning" something during the course of the activity may lower defenses and incorporates an additional component of playfulness to the technique.

In addition to writing the positive and negative statements on the index cards, the therapist draws a happy face and writes "Positive Thoughts" on one sheet of paper and a sad face with the words "Negative Thoughts" on the other. The papers are hung on opposite walls or in a manner that separates the two concepts.

To facilitate the client's understanding of the interplay between thoughts, feelings, and behaviors, the therapist leads a discussion regarding the fact that the way a person thinks about their problems can make the person feel "better" or "worse." These feelings then influence our behaviors. Thoughts that make us feel "better" are called positive thoughts, and thoughts that make us feel "worse" are called negative thoughts.

The child and therapist brainstorm emotions associated with feeling "better." As these emotions are brainstormed, the therapist writes the emotions on the paper labeled "Positive Thoughts." Next, emotions associated with feeling "worse" are brainstormed and written on the paper labeled "Negative Thoughts." Possible emotions associated with feeling "better" or "worse" are delineated on the following pages. This list is intended to serve only as a guide. The actual list of emotions generated during the activity will reflect the client's cognitive and developmental level. A discussion pertaining to the connection between positive thoughts that make us feel better versus negative thoughts that make us feel worse is facilitated.

Following this discussion, the therapist and client take turns selecting index cards and determining whether the statement on the card is a positive thought or a negative thought. When selecting cards, players read the statement silently, determine if the statement is positive or negative, and then read the statement out loud using the tone of voice and facial expression that reflects how the thought would make the person feel. The player tapes the card onto the corresponding paper designating the statement as either a "Positive Thought" or a "Negative Thought." If a player selects a card with "Treat," "Sticker," or a smiley face, he or she selects a piece of candy, sticker, or other small prize (optional).

After all the cards have been selected, a discussion about behaviors an individual may engage in after thinking positive thoughts can be initiated. The central premise of this therapeutic discussion should emphasize the interplay of thoughts, feelings, and behaviors and encourage the use of positive cognitions which may lead to more constructive, helpful choices and behavior.

The client is encouraged to select two to three positive thoughts to utilize in between sessions. If clinically appropriate, the parent or caregiver can be included at the end of the session so the client can explain the concept of positive and negative thinking and tell the caregiver the positive thoughts the client will attempt to utilize in between sessions. The caregiver should be encouraged to reinforce and model the identified positive cognitions to assist in generalization of this therapeutic concept.

For clients who are confronting a specific presenting problem such as divorce, bereavement, or abuse, this intervention can be utilized during subsequent sessions to focus on specific maladaptive cognitions pertaining to the identified problem with an emphasis on identifying and generating alternative, more adaptive cognitions to replace maladaptive ones.

Feelings Associated with "*Feeling Better*"

- Happy
- Hopeful
- Confident
- Proud
- Brave
- Calm
- Content
- Satisfied
- Optimistic
- Relieved
- Composed
- Settled
- Tranquil
- Relaxed
- Capable
- At ease
- Determined
- Inspired
- Joyful

Feelings Associated with "*Feeling Worse*"

- Hopeless
- Gloomy
- Dreary
- Scared
- Distressed
- Insecure
- Troubled

- Overwhelmed
- Stressed
- Worried
- Sad
- Mad
- Discouraged
- Frustrated
- Jealous
- Lonely
- Depressed
- Upset
- Uncomfortable
- Angry

General Positive Thoughts

- I tried my best.
- It's going to be okay.
- I'll try harder next time.
- I'm not going to give up.
- I can do it.
- I don't have to be perfect.
- I can handle this.
- I will learn from my mistakes.
- I can make it through this.
- I believe in myself.
- Be strong.
- I'm not going to let this get to me.
- It will all work out in the end.
- I'm not going to make a big deal out of this.
- Someday, things will get better.
- I'm going to keep hanging in there.
- I can handle whatever comes my way.

General Negative Thoughts

- Things will never get better.
- Nothing I do ever works out.
- I never win.
- I can't do this.
- I'm no good at this.
- This is too hard.
- I never get what I want.
- Nobody likes me.
- This is stupid.

- Why even try?
- Bad things always happen to me.
- I can't take this anymore.
- I hate my life.
- One of these days, I'm just going to crack.
- I wish I was someone else.
- Nothing I do matters.
- Everyone else is better than me.

Chapter 4: ADHD

Attention-Deficit Hyperactivity Disorder (ADHD) is a common treatment issue for practitioners working with children, adolescents, and families. Treatment of ADHD involves a multimodal approach and generally includes pharmacological and classroom-based interventions along with parental psychoeducation and training. However, it is additionally important to recognize that difficulties associated with ADHD extend beyond the primary symptoms of inattention, hyperactivity, and impulsivity and can result in social skills deficits, poor academic performance, and social rejection. Although the use of psychotropic medication, classroom interventions, and parent psychoeducation are part of the treatment of ADHD, these interventions may be insufficient in addressing the skill-building this population needs. Subsequently, techniques in this chapter directly target symptoms associated with ADHD and attempt to provide skills to minimize the impact of inattention, hyperactivity, and impulsivity. Interventions can be utilized in individual therapy, with families, or incorporated into group programs or curriculum.

Since it is ineffective for clients to merely learn, utilize, and practice the skills addressed through these techniques during a therapy session, generalization is crucial to the success of these interventions. Techniques will be most effective if the acquired skills are reinforced by the therapist, parents, and other individuals in the client's support system. Incorporating structured homework assignments for each intervention in which clients and caregivers practice the therapeutic skills in natural settings and report their progress to the therapist will facilitate rehearsal and generalization, which are essential for change.

Since clinical levels of inattention, hyperactivity, and impulsivity may be present for individuals who are not diagnosed with ADHD, interventions contained in this chapter can be utilized to target symptom reduction even when full diagnostic criteria for the disorder is not met. In addition, it is important to be mindful of the fact that ADHD can be over and/or misdiagnosed. Symptoms that appear to be indicative of ADHD might actually be clinical indicators of another disorder, such as Posttraumatic Stress Disorder (PTSD) or an anxiety disorder. Ensuring assessment is an ongoing process, gathering information from collateral sources, and obtaining a thorough psychosocial history may assist in this differential diagnosis.

The Simon Game

Intervention Summary

This intervention is a modified version of the handheld electronic game Simon® (Hasbro). The game is played according to the typical rules of play with the additional rule that if a player is unsuccessful at imitating the series of lights and sounds made by Simon®, the player selects and responds to a game card. The game cards address different components of ADHD and focus on skill development in areas related to symptoms of the disorder.

Purpose

- Increase attention span
- Facilitate self-control
- Reduce impulsivity
- Facilitate an understanding of ADHD and the associated symptoms

Modality

- Individual
- Group
- Family

Age Range

- 7–12 years

Materials

- Simon® electronic game (Hasbro) or a free on-line memory game (i.e. Concentration, Simon, etc.) or an I SPY© book or game (Scholastic)
- Game cards (see attached)
- Small candy (Jolly Ranchers™, Hershey Kisses™, etc.) or stickers

Preparation

Prior to the game, the attached game cards need to be written on index cards.

Description

This intervention is a modified version of the handheld electronic game Simon® (Hasbro). The game entails "Simon" producing a series of lights and sounds, which a player must successfully imitate to win the round. If the Simon® game is not available, a free on-line memory game, such as Concentration, can be utilized instead. Free on-line games can be accessed by typing "memory games for children" or other key words into an internet search engine. An additional modification would be to use an "I SPY"© (Scholastic) book or game with a time limit for players to locate identified items.

For this technique, Simon® is played according to the regular rules of play with the additional rule that if a player is unsuccessful at imitating the game, the player selects and responds to a game card. (See the following pages for game cards.) Each card addresses a different component of ADHD including such things as skill development in areas related to symptoms of ADHD and psychoeducation.

During the course of play, if a player is successful at imitating the game, he or she selects a treat, sticker, or other small prize. Although this is an optional part of the intervention, the prospect of "winning" something during the course of the activity may lower defenses and incorporates an additional component of playfulness into the technique.

The very nature of the Simon® game requires players to focus their attention in order to successfully duplicate Simon's pattern of sounds and lights. The game cards create an additional therapeutic component as the concepts addressed through the cards target skills needed to mediate symptoms of inattention, hyperactivity, and impulsivity. Throughout the activity, the therapist has the opportunity to normalize and validate the experiences identified and discussed by the child.

Therapeutic Questions for the "Simon" Game

- What does Attention-Deficit Hyperactivity Disorder (ADHD) mean?

- What is something you can do to help you pay attention in school?

- Listening is an important skill. Listen to someone tell a story and summarize the story.

- Practice running in place in very slow motion for one minute.

- Why is it important to think before you do something?

- Being organized and planning ahead are important skills. Practice these skills by making an after-school schedule.

- What makes it hard for you to pay attention?

- Practice sitting as still as you can for two minutes.

- Everyone has things they are good at and things they are not so good at. What is one thing you are good at and one thing you are not so good at?

- Tell about a time you got in trouble at home or school. What can you do differently next time?

- Sometimes it is hard for children who have ADHD to make friends. Practice inviting someone to play with you.

- Talk about something you can do to help you stop and think before you do something.

- What is one way your ADHD affects you and what can you do to make this better?

- Talk about something you would like to accomplish in the next one to two months and discuss what steps you will take to reach your goal.

- After we have a bad day, it is hard to get back on track. What is something positive you can say to yourself at the beginning of the next day to help start the day off feeling good?

What's Different?

Intervention Summary

This intervention focuses on developing skills to expand the client's attention span and reduce impulsivity. Doll furniture or Matchbox® cars and road signs are arranged to create a "scene" that the client studies. The client turns around, something in the scene is rearranged, and the client turns back around and identifies the change. As the intervention progresses, the number and complexity of the changes made to the scene can be increased. The therapist and client switch roles throughout the technique, allowing the therapist to provide a coping model for the client to learn new skills.

Purpose

- Develop strategies to increase attention span
- Develop strategies to increase concentration

Modality

- Individual
- Group
- Family

Age Range

- 5–12 years

Materials

- Doll furniture or Matchbox® cars and road signs
- Masking tape

Description

For this intervention, the child is challenged to focus his or her attention and identify changes made to a "scene" created using either doll furniture or Matchbox® cars and road signs. The masking tape is used to mark off an area to represent the "scene." The furniture or cars and road signs are placed in the "scene" and the child is instructed to pay attention to where each item is placed. After the child has studied the scene, the child turns around and the therapist makes one change to the scene (i.e. removing an item, adding an item, changing the location of an item, etc.). The child is then instructed to turn back around and identify what has changed. The therapist should begin by making a change that is clear and obvious and gradually make more challenging changes as clinically indicated. Pacing the difficulty of the changes made to the scene reduces the likelihood that the child will become frustrated at the onset of the intervention.

The therapist and child switch roles with the child arranging and changing the scene and the therapist identifying what has been changed. This provides an opportunity for the therapist to provide a coping model to demonstrate skills necessary to successfully identify changes. For example, the therapist can deliberately be distracted by extraneous stimuli. By thinking out loud, recognizing this, and correcting the inattentive behavior using skills to remain attentive, the therapist provides the child with the opportunity to learn new skills as the therapist attempts to master the task at hand.

As the intervention progresses, the number of changes and complexity of the changes made to the scene can be increased.

This intervention provides the opportunity for the therapist to reinforce attentive behavior as well as model skills necessary to remain on-task. The child and therapist can discuss ways the child can generalize these skills and attentive behavior to environments outside of the therapeutic setting. Use of this intervention also places responsibility for managing ADHD behaviors onto the child and creates an opportunity to empower and motivate children to take responsibility for skill development in these areas.

This intervention can be modified for adolescents by using another media instead of doll furniture and Matchbox® cars and road signs. For example, baseball cards or video game covers can be used instead.

Fast Play-Slow Play

Intervention Summary

This intervention is a modified version of the board game Memory® (Milton Bradley) and allows the client to experience the consequences of inattentive, impulsive behavior versus the benefits of focused, controlled behavior. The game Memory® is played twice. The first game is played by turning cards over as quickly as possible without thinking about which cards to turn or trying to remember where the matches are located. The second game is played using concentration and strategy prior to turning cards over. The consequences of playing fast and haphazardly versus the benefits of playing slow and controlled are explored.

Purpose

- Increase attention span
- Develop self-control
- Explore the consequences of impulsive and inattentive behavior

Modality

- Individual

Age Range

- 5–12 years

Materials

- Memory Game® (Milton Bradley)

Description

This intervention is a modified version of the board game Memory® (Milton Bradley) and allows the child to experience the consequences of inattentive, impulsive behavior versus the benefits of focused, controlled behavior. The Memory® game is a simple matching game where players turn over two cards at a time in an attempt to locate matching pairs.

This therapeutic version requires that the Memory® game be played twice. Therefore, prior to beginning, the game cards are separated into two sets of matching pairs. The first game is played using the regular rules of play with the additional rule that players are instructed to turn over cards as quickly as possible without thinking about which cards to turn or trying to remember where the matches are located.

After the game is played using this format, the child and therapist discuss how mistakes were made and successful matching of pairs was difficult due to the inattentive, impulsive behavior each player exhibited.

The game is then played a second time with the remaining set of matching pairs. However, this time, each player is instructed to concentrate and use strategy prior to turning cards over. During this version of the game, players should experience more success at obtaining matches due to the fact that they are focusing their attention and controlling their behavior as opposed to impulsively turning over cards.

Following both games, the therapist and child discuss the difference between playing the game in a slow, controlled manner versus impulsively turning cards over. The consequences of playing fast and haphazardly versus the benefits of playing slow and controlled can be explored in the context of the intervention. Specific strategies the child utilized during the "slow play" portion of the intervention should be identified and discussed. As part of this discussion, generalization of these skills and strategies should be conducted.

As the strategies are identified, the therapist or child writes these strategies on a piece of paper. After the intervention is complete, the child can decorate the paper to create a poster of strategies the child can use to remain attentive and controlled. The poster serves as a transitional object and a strategy to increase generalization of the skills identified through the technique.

If clinically appropriate, the poster can be reviewed with the caregiver at the end of the session. The caregiver should be encouraged to reinforce and model the strategies in between sessions as well.

Since many children with ADHD can become frustrated with this type of activity, it is important that the therapist introduce the activity in a playful and engaging manner and reinforce that the purpose of the activity is to practice moving too fast and practice moving slowly to understand the difference and develop strategies to help the client develop more control. Since the therapist participates in the activity alongside the client, this may normalize the process and reduce the child's frustration level.

Chapter 5: Self-Esteem

A substantial portion of children, adolescents, and families who have contact with mental health practitioners struggle with issues related to self-esteem. These issues may be a part of the clinical diagnosis, as with some forms of depression, or may be secondary to abuse, trauma or other presenting problems. Regardless of the origin, improving self-esteem is an important part of clinical work. When individuals are able to recognize their strengths and self-worth, they are better able to regulate their emotions, interact more positively with others, and manage their reactions to problems and stressors more productively. Interventions included in this chapter can be utilized to help clients identify positive self-attributes and strengths, and subsequently, strengthen their self-esteem.

For individuals with a particularly low or damaged self-esteem, interventions may need to be gradually utilized to assist the individual in tolerating positive statements about themselves. For younger children, techniques in this chapter will provide a means to make the concept of self-esteem more concrete.

Caregiver involvement is crucial to enhance self-esteem. Subsequently, incorporating caregivers into the activities in this chapter will assist in achieving greater therapeutic gains while providing a unique opportunity for the caregiver to identify and validate their child's positive attributes.

Super Star!

Intervention Summary

This intervention focuses on helping clients identify positive self-traits and attributes using creative arts media. The Look It's Me Star™ (Oriental Trading Company) is decorated by the client with words, symbols, or drawings to represent the client's positive self-traits.

Purpose

- Improve self-esteem
- Identify positive self-attributes
- Create a concrete representation of self-esteem

Modality

- Individual
- Group
- Family

Age Range

- 5–18 years

Materials

- "Look It's Me Stars" by Hands on Fun™ (Oriental Trading Company)
- Picture of child or Polaroid™ camera
- Paper
- Writing and drawing utensils (i.e. markers, crayons, colored pencils, etc.)
- Miscellaneous art supplies such as glitter, glue, etc. (optional)

Description

This intervention focuses on assisting clients in identifying positive self-traits and attributes using creative arts media. The "Look It's Me Star" from Oriental Trading Company™ is a star-shaped cardboard picture frame with a cut-out center for a photograph. For this intervention, the "Look It's Me Star"™ will be decorated by the client with words, symbols, or drawings to represent the client's positive self-traits.

The session begins with a general discussion about self-esteem. The therapist explains that self-esteem is the way people feel about themselves and includes personal qualities that describe a person. A distinction should be made between superficial and materialistic possessions and belongings versus personal traits and characteristics. The therapist explains a person's self-esteem isn't related to the way the person's hair looks or the type of clothes he or she wears, but on the things that make the person unique and special. These are things that are on the inside of a person. For younger children, an alternative explanation might be, "Self-esteem includes the things that make us special and help us be a good friend."

Together, the client and therapist brainstorm characteristics that might make up a person's self-esteem. As this list of traits is generated, the therapist writes the identified characteristics and traits on a sheet of paper. This list can be used by the client later in the intervention when the client identifies his or her personal positive traits.

Traits and attributes will be more concrete for younger children and will become more complex and abstract for older children and adolescents. Possible positive self-traits and attributes for younger children might include such things as being kind, nice, friendly, good at sharing, smart, hard working, honest, polite, funny, and good at following directions. Possible positive self-traits and attributes for older children and adolescents might include such things as being trustworthy, compassionate, loyal, dedicated, optimistic, motivated, creative, committed, considerate, and devoted.

After the list of personal characteristics is generated, the client is instructed to select five or more traits that describe the client to represent parts of the client's self-esteem. The drawing and art materials are used by the client to create their own star, which represents their identified traits. This can be as simple or as elaborate as the client wants and can consist of writing the traits on the stars, using glitter or other art media, or drawing pictures or symbols to represent the identified traits. The completed star can be taken home as a transitional object, which serves to remind the client of the positive self-attributes identified during the activity.

If possible, have the client bring a photograph to the session. If a photograph is not available, the therapist can take a picture of the client. This is best done with a Polaroid™ camera as this will produce an instant picture. If this is not possible, the therapist will need to take a photograph of the client prior to the session and have the picture developed. Another option would be for the client to complete his or her star and have the photograph added the following session after the therapist has it developed.

After the client has completed his or her self-esteem star, the photograph of the client is taped to the backside of the star. This creates the completed activity and represents the "star" qualities of the client complete with a visual representation of the client.

The completed project is processed with the client. The therapist has the opportunity to validate the positive attributes identified by the client as well as share some of the positive attributes the therapist has observed in the client.

If appropriate, the therapist and client can share the star with the caregiver. The caregiver should be encouraged to support the client's identified positive self-traits.

If utilized in a group or family setting, a modification might include members in the session adding positive attributes they have noticed to each others' respective stars.

The star provides a tangible representation of self-esteem and makes this approach developmentally appropriate for younger children whose thought processes are more concrete. The focus on positive characteristics directly targets the area of self-esteem. This is especially helpful due to the fact that individuals receiving therapy or counseling are generally over-focused on negative aspects of themselves or the problems they are dealing with, and subsequently, often struggle to see the positive traits they possess. This intervention can assist in building a foundation to help facilitate a cognitive shift in which the client begins to focus on his or her positive self-traits as opposed to negative ones. With individuals who have a trauma history, emphasizing positive self-attributes can result in the individual feeling empowered and can help them acknowledge their resilience in overcoming adversity.

I Can't Be Blown Away

Intervention Summary

To assist clients in identifying their positive self-traits and attributes, clients design a pinwheel that identifies four of their positive self-traits. The metaphor for the intervention is that the client has qualities that can keep the child strong even during rough, stormy times. In that manner, the client "can't be blown away" by problems or obstacles.

Purpose

- Improve self-esteem
- Identify positive self-attributes
- Explore how positive traits and characteristics can provide support during difficult times

Modality

- Individual
- Group
- Family

Age Range

- 5–12 years

Materials

- Design Your Own Paper Pinwheel by Hands On Fun™ (Oriental Trading Company)
- Writing and drawing utensils (i.e. markers, crayons, colored pencils, etc.)
- Miscellaneous art supplies such as glitter, glue, etc. (optional)

Description

This intervention focuses on helping clients identify positive self-traits and characteristics as an avenue to enhance self-confidence and improve self-esteem. The metaphor for the technique centers on the concept of being "blown away" by problems, circumstances, and situations and the fact that a person's positive traits and characteristics can help them survive and persevere during difficult times.

The session begins with a general discussion regarding self-esteem. The therapist explains that self-esteem is the way people feel about themselves and includes personal qualities that describe a person. A distinction should be made between superficial and materialistic possessions and belongings versus personal traits and characteristics. The therapist explains a person's self-esteem is not related to the way the person's hair looks or the type of clothes he or she wears, but on the things that make the person unique and special. These are things that are inside the person.

Together, the client and therapist brainstorm characteristics that might comprise a person's self-esteem. As this list of traits is generated, the therapist writes the identified characteristics and traits on a sheet of paper. This list can be used by the client later in the intervention when the client identifies his or her own positive traits.

During this discussion, the concept of having both strengths and weaknesses should be normalized. The client should recognize that a person does not have to be perfect or possess all the positive traits generated on the list. The key is to recognize your own individual strengths and understand how to use these strengths during times of need.

Traits and attributes will be more concrete for younger children and will become more complex and abstract for older children and adolescents. Possible positive self-traits and attributes for younger children might include such things as being kind, nice, friendly, good at sharing, smart, hard working, honest, polite, funny, and good at following directions. Possible positive self-traits and attributes for older children and adolescents might include such things as being trustworthy, compassionate, loyal, dedicated, optimistic, motivated, creative, committed, considerate, and devoted.

After the list of characteristics and traits is generated, the client is instructed to select four traits that describe the client to represent the client's self-esteem. These four traits are written, drawn, or symbolically represented on the four petals of the pinwheel. This can be as simple or as elaborate as the client wants and can consist of writing the traits, drawing pictures or symbols to represent the traits, or using glitter or other art media. The child then decorates the pinwheel using the drawing and art materials.

When the pinwheel is complete, the therapist challenges the client to "blow away" the positive traits. Naturally, no matter how hard the client blows, the positive qualities do not get "blown away." Similarly, a discussion should ensue pertaining to perseverance during turbulent times and when confronting problems and difficulties by remembering positive self-attributes and utilizing these strengths.

As the completed project is processed with the client, the therapist has the opportunity to validate the positive attributes identified by the client as well as share some of the positive attributes the therapist has observed in the client.

The pinwheel can be taken home to serve as a transitional object that will remind the client of the positive traits identified during the session. If appropriate, the therapist and child can show the pinwheel to the caregiver. The caregiver should be encouraged to validate the child's identified positive self-traits.

If utilized in a group or family setting, a modification might include members in the session adding positive attributes they have noticed to each others' respective projects.

The pinwheel provides a tangible representation of self-esteem and makes this approach developmentally appropriate for younger children whose thought processes are more concrete. The focus on positive characteristics directly targets the area of self-esteem and the metaphor of not being able to blow the positive self-traits away helps facilitate an understanding of the enduring nature of these attributes. This is especially helpful due to the fact that individuals receiving therapy or counseling are generally over-focused on negative aspects of themselves or the problems they are dealing with, and subsequently, often struggle to see the positive traits they possess. This intervention can assist in building a foundation to help facilitate a cognitive shift in which clients begin to focus on their positive self-traits as opposed to negative attributes. For individuals with a trauma history, this can serve as an avenue to explore their resiliency and serve as a springboard to explore how their ability to overcome adversity may serve them later in life.

I Have Heart

Intervention Summary

The phrase "having heart" provides the foundation for clients to identify positive self-traits. Players take turns rolling a pair of dice. If a player rolls doubles, he or she selects a treat, sticker, or other small prize. If the player rolls any other combination of numbers, the player must finish the sentence "I have heart because…" Players complete the sentence by identifying a positive self-attribute.

Purpose

- Identify positive self-attributes
- Improve self-esteem

Modality

- Individual
- Group
- Family

Age Range

- 7 years–Adults

Materials

- Dice
- Small candy (Jolly Ranchers™, Hershey Kisses™, etc.) or stickers (optional)

Description

This intervention uses a game format to assist clients in identifying positive self-traits and attributes. All that is needed for this technique is a set of dice.

The concept of "having heart" provides the foundation for this intervention. The therapist and client discuss the meaning of this phrase with the therapist explaining that when someone has "heart" it means he or she has drive and motivation inside of them that helps them accomplish tasks and carries them through difficult, adverse times. For young children, a modified explanation might be, "Having heart refers to all the things about us that make us special." The therapist explains that "having heart" is another way to describe positive self-traits. These positive traits are things that make us feel confident and shape our self-esteem. When discussing the concept of self-esteem, a distinction should be made between superficial and materialistic possessions and belongings versus personal traits and characteristics. The therapist explains a person's self-esteem is not related to the way the person's hair looks or the type of clothes he or she wears, but on the things that make the person unique and special.

The therapist explains this activity is going to help players identify the positive things inside of them that make them "have heart." During the game, players take turns rolling the dice. If a player rolls doubles, he or she selects a treat, sticker, or other small prize. Although this is an optional part of the intervention, the prospect of "winning" something during the course of the game may lower defenses and incorporates an additional component of playfulness to the intervention.

If the player rolls any other combination of numbers, the player must finish the sentence, "I have heart because..." Players complete this sentence by identifying a positive self-attribute.

Traits and attributes will be more concrete for younger children and will become more complex and abstract for older children and adolescents. Possible positive self-traits and attributes for younger children might include such things as being kind, friendly, good at sharing, smart, hard working, honest, polite, funny, and good at following directions. Possible positive self-traits and attributes for older children and adolescents might include such things as being trustworthy, compassionate, loyal, dedicated, optimistic, motivated, creative, committed, and devoted.

If used in individual therapy, the therapist plays the game with the client. If utilized in a group or family session, the therapist has the option of playing along or serving as a facilitator of the game. When the therapist participates, the therapist's responses should reflect developmentally appropriate concepts as this may facilitate similar responses from the client. For example, if this intervention is being used with a five-year-old, the therapist might say, "I have heart because I am good at waiting my turn" or "I have heart because I am nice." If being played with a 16-year-old, the therapist might finish the sentence with a more complex concept, such as being determined, considerate, or tolerant of differences.

As play progresses, the processing component of this intervention can be expanded by adding additional components to the sentence "I have heart because..." One way to accomplish this is to have players include examples of a time they used the quality they identified such as, "I have heart because I am caring. For example, when my friend was sad I hugged her and told her things would be okay." If used in a group or family setting, another way to increase the processing component of this technique is to have people start to identify reasons they feel others "have heart." For example, "I think my mom has heart because she is determined. For example, she went back to school to get her degree so she could get a better job." Having caregivers identify and explain reasons their child has "heart" is helpful in strengthening the parent-child relationship and focusing on positive aspects of the child as opposed to emphasizing problems and areas of difficulty.

During the course of play, the therapist has the opportunity to validate the positive attributes identified by the client. As the traits are identified during the course of the game, the therapist can write the traits on a piece of paper. After the game is complete, the client can decorate the paper to create a poster representing the qualities that give the client "heart." The poster serves as a transitional object to reinforce these traits. If clinically appropriate, the poster can be reviewed with the caregiver at the end of the session. The caregiver should be encouraged to validate the child's identified positive self-traits.

This technique provides a structured opportunity to focus on positive self-traits. The game format makes this approach developmentally appropriate for younger children. The focus on positive characteristics directly targets the area of self-esteem. This is especially helpful due to the fact that individuals receiving therapy or counseling are generally over-focused on negative aspects of themselves or the problems they are dealing with, and subsequently, often struggle to see the positive traits they possess. This intervention can assist in building a foundation to help facilitate a cognitive shift in which the client begins to focus on his or her positive self-traits as opposed to negative attributes.

Chapter 6: Interpersonal Boundaries

Many practitioners working with children, adolescents, and families are familiar with clients who are physically intrusive and unable to remain within their own personal space. These individuals face many challenges including social rejection, isolation, and even possible victimization. Subsequently, a portion of the practitioner's work often focuses on defining and strengthening interpersonal boundaries.

Since the concept of interpersonal space is multidimensional, interventions in this chapter address boundaries from different perspectives including developing strategies to remain within one's own personal space, developing strategies to let others know they are in your personal space, and making decisions regarding disclosing personal or private information. For young children, the techniques in this chapter strive to provide a concrete representation of personal space.

My Boundary Bubbles

Intervention Summary

This intervention provides a concrete representation of personal boundaries along with several strategies to maintain appropriate interpersonal space. Cross-stitch hoops serve to create "boundary bubbles" around a graphic of a child figure. Each cross-stitch hoop is traced around the image and labeled with a strategy to assist the child in remaining in his or her own space. By the time the child has identified a strategy for each hoop, the image on the paper is surrounded with different "boundary bubbles" that define personal space and provide practical strategies to strengthen interpersonal boundaries.

Purpose

- Develop an improved sense of personal space
- Develop concrete strategies to respect, maintain, and strengthen interpersonal boundaries

Modality

- Individual
- Group
- Family

Age Range

- 5–11 years

Materials

- Several cross-stitch hoops of various sizes
- 8½ x 11 paper with graphics of children in the middle (see attached)
- Drawing/writing materials (colored pencils, markers, etc.)
- Hula-hoop (optional)

Description

Many children experience difficulty maintaining and respecting personal boundaries. There are many factors that may contribute to this including such things as impulsivity or a history of abuse. It is often difficult and challenging to help children understand the concept of personal space and develop strategies for keeping their hands and feet to themselves. This intervention provides children with a concrete representation of personal space along with several strategies to utilize to maintain appropriate interpersonal boundaries.

The intervention begins by discussing the concept of personal space. One metaphor that can be utilized to explain personal space would be to describe personal space as an invisible hula-hoop that separates people from each other. An actual hula-hoop can be used to demonstrate the existence of personal space. The therapist and child discuss the importance of respecting the personal space of others just as other people should respect our personal space. A discussion should ensue regarding ways personal space can be violated such as grabbing things away from someone, sitting too close to another person, touching someone without permission, taking someone's personal belongings without permission, or becoming physically aggressive such as pushing or hitting.

The child is told that this activity will help him or her respect the personal space of others by learning ways to stay in the child's own personal space. The child selects a piece of paper with a graphic of a small child printed in the center. Graphics can be obtained from various software programs or downloaded from a variety of websites. The graphic must be small enough to fit inside the smallest cross-stitch hoop. A series of graphics from Microsoft Office have been included on the following pages for the purpose of this intervention. The cross-stitch hoops are placed on the table with the hoops arranged one inside the other. During the activity, each hoop is traced around the graphic, one hoop inside of another, beginning with the smallest hoop. Every hoop creates a "boundary bubble" that serves to represent a different strategy for the child to utilize to remain within his or her own personal space.

The child starts by selecting the smallest hoop, placing it around the graphic, tracing the hoop around the image, and labeling the circle he or she has drawn with a strategy to assist the child in remaining in his or her own space. This process is repeated for each cross-stitch hoop. By the time the child has identified a strategy for each hoop, the image on the paper is surrounded with different "boundary bubbles," which define personal space and provide practical strategies to strengthen interpersonal boundaries.

The process of identifying various strategies to respect the personal space of others may be difficult for the child, and subsequently, may require substantial involvement from the therapist. Strategies may include such things as, "Ask before touching," "Don't take things without permission," "Ask before hugging," "Knock and wait before opening a closed door," and "Don't touch people without permission." In addition, simple "stop and think" statements can be generated such as, "Keep my hands to myself" or "Stay in my space." For older children, more complex boundaries can be explored such as "Don't dress in a way that shows too much of my body," "Be careful who I tell my business to," and "Keep the door closed when getting dressed." For younger children, having a list of strategies for the child to choose from might assist in the process of creating the "boundary bubbles."

To provide the child with the opportunity to practice the identified strategies, puppets can be used to act out the strategies. Both the therapist and child take turns using the puppets to practice the identified strategies. This gives the therapist the chance to model the skills as well as provide feedback to the child. This component of behavioral rehearsal may increase the likelihood the child will utilize the skills in settings beyond the therapeutic environment.

The completed project serves as a visual reminder of the various strategies the child can utilize to remain within his or her own personal space. The child can be given the homework assignment to practice using the skills identified through the technique and report progress to the therapist. If clinically appropriate, the completed activity can be reviewed with the caregiver at the end of the session. The caregiver should be encouraged to reinforce and model the strategies identified through the intervention.

This intervention presents a concrete representation of personal space, provides a transitional object to assist with generalization, and assists the child in developing practical strategies to remain within his or her personal space.

Respect My Space

Intervention Summary

Recognizing the multidimensional nature of interpersonal boundaries, this technique focuses on developing assertive statements and behaviors the client can utilize when others are too close to them. The client creates a hula-hoop using sections of the Build-Your-Own Activity Hoop™ (Oriental Trading Company). As the hula-hoop is constructed, each section serves to represent a different assertive statement or behavior to communicate that others are in the client's personal space.

Purpose

- Develop assertive communication skills to improve interpersonal boundaries
- Develop concrete strategies to respect, maintain, and strengthen interpersonal boundaries
- Provide behavioral rehearsal of skills related to assertive communication and personal space

Modality

- Individual
- Group
- Family

Age Range

- 5–11 years

Materials

- Make Your Own Activity Hoops™ (Oriental Trading Company) or a hula-hoop cut into six sections
- Paper
- Writing utensil

Description

The abstract concept of personal space is often difficult for children to understand and operationalize. Poor interpersonal boundaries can be related to a number of factors including such things as impulsivity, poor social skills, or a history of abuse. Children served by mental health professionals frequently experience significant difficulties utilizing appropriate interpersonal boundaries. Subsequently, practitioners need interventions to address and strengthen this area. Since interpersonal boundaries are multidimensional, not only do interventions need to focus on helping children remain in their own personal space, but techniques also need to focus on helping children communicate when other people are in their space. This intervention helps children develop and rehearse assertive statements and behaviors that let others know they are too close to the child.

During the session, the child constructs a hula-hoop using the Make Your Own Activity Hoop™ from Oriental Trading Company. The Make Your Own Activity Hoop™ contains colored pieces of a hula-hoop that are cut into sections and can be connected together to create a larger hula-hoop. For this technique, the individual pieces of the Make Your Own Activity Hoop™ are used to create the child's personal space with each section of the hula-hoop serving as an assertive statement or behavior that the child can utilize to communicate that someone is too close to him or her. The Make Your Own Activity Hoop™ costs approximately $20.00 for a set of 50 pieces. If the Make Your Own Activity Hoop™ is not available, a regular hula-hoop can be cut into six pieces, which will be reassembled during the course of the activity.

The intervention begins by discussing the concept of personal space. A hula-hoop can be used to demonstrate the existence of personal space. The therapist and child discuss the importance of not only respecting the personal space of others, but of having other people respect our personal space as well.

The child is told this activity will help him or her develop polite ways of communicating when other people are too close to them or are in their personal space. The child is given five to six pieces of the Make Your Own Activity Hoop™ from which he or she will build a personal hula-hoop. Each section of the hoop serves as an assertive strategy to communicate that someone is too close to the child. Prior to attaching each piece of the hoop together, the child will identify one strategy to let others know that they are too close to the child. As the child identifies the various strategies, the therapist writes the ideas down to create a list of strategies the child has identified. After the intervention is complete, the child can decorate the paper to create a poster to serve as a transitional object to increase generalization of skills identified through the technique.

The process of identifying assertive statements and strategies to communicate when others are in the child's personal space may be difficult for the child, and subsequently, may require substantial involvement from the therapist. Assertive statements that communicate someone is too close to another person can include such things as, "Excuse me, you're too close to me," "Can you move over a little?" or "Would you please back up?" Behaviors that communicate a person is too close might include such things as taking a step backward or holding a hand out in front of you as if to communicate "Stop."

After the child identifies five to six different strategies, one strategy for each section of the hula-hoop, the child then practices each strategy. In this portion of the intervention, the child stands inside the "Respect My Space" hula-hoop they just created and the therapist begins to walk toward the child. When the therapist gets too close, the child utilizes one of the strategies identified through the creation of the hula-hoop. This continues until the child has rehearsed each identified strategy. As the child rehearses these skills, the therapist provides feedback and reinforcement. This component of behavioral rehearsal is essential as behavioral rehearsal is one of the best ways to learn and acquire new skills.

If appropriate and possible, the caregiver should be included at the end of the session to learn the strategies and observe the child rehearsing the skills. The caregiver can even participate in the behavioral rehearsal component of the technique if clinically indicated and appropriate. Since families can also lack appropriate boundaries, this intervention can be modified for use in family sessions with family members taking turns identifying appropriate family boundaries (i.e. "Knock before entering," "Close the door when in the bathroom," "Ask permission before using someone's things," etc.).

This technique utilizes several components that are effective in working with children including providing a concrete representation of personal space, creating a transitional object to assist with generalization, and providing the opportunity to rehearse the therapeutic skills.

Although this intervention can be utilized across populations, it is particularly useful for sexually abused children as sexual abuse impedes directly on a child's personal space and often results in poor interpersonal boundaries. In addition to strengthening personal boundaries, this technique also focuses on increasing assertive communication skills. For children with a history of sexual abuse, this is an important area of skill-building and may reduce potential future victimization.

Who, What, Where, and When

Intervention Summary

This technique, which is useful for highly sensitive presenting problems, assists clients in differentiating between appropriate situations to discuss private information and situations in which it might be best to wait. Players take turns selecting index cards with different places and situations written on them. If the player decides the situation or place is an appropriate time to discuss the identified problem, the card is taped on a page labeled "Good Time." If the player decides the situation or place is a time in which it might be best to wait to talk about the identified problem, the card is taped on a page labeled "Time to Wait."

Purpose

- Strengthen interpersonal boundaries by developing discretion when discussing private information
- Discriminate between situations in which it is appropriate to discuss personal information and situations in which it might be best to wait

Modality

- Individual
- Group
- Family

Age Range

- 7–16 years

Materials

- 8 ½ x 11 paper or flip chart
- Marker
- Tape
- Index cards
- Small candy or stickers (optional)

Description

Practitioners often encounter children, adolescents, and families struggling with highly sensitive stressors and presenting problems including such things as sexual abuse, parental incarceration, or AIDS. Although treatment focuses on processing these issues, treatment may also need to focus on assisting clients in discriminating between appropriate situations to discuss these matters and times in which it might be in the client's best interest to wait.

Due to the fact that interpersonal boundaries are multidimensional, this intervention focuses on addressing and strengthening boundaries from the perspective of protecting private information and reaching out to your support system as opposed to indiscriminately discussing private matters.

This intervention was originally designed for victims of sexual abuse and is based on research that suggests highly emotional reactions, disbelief, and nonsupport have a powerful influence on a victim's post-disclosure experience and may significantly impact the victim's understanding of the abuse, his or her self-image, and the victim's ability to trust others (Deblinger & Heflin, 1996). Since these types of reactions may accompany indiscriminate discussions of the sexual abuse, this technique was originally developed to strengthen interpersonal boundaries in regard to discussing the abuse with the victim's support system or with individuals in a position to offer appropriate support to the victim versus randomly discussing this information with others. Since its inception, this technique has been successfully used with other highly stigmatized presenting problems including emotionally charged issues such as serious criminal charges against a family member, circumstances surrounding contentious divorces, or sensitive health conditions.

Prior to the session, different scenarios, settings, or situations the client may encounter are written on index cards. A list of possible situations and circumstances is included on the following page to serve as a guide. The scenarios written on the index cards will likely vary from client to client and should be based on the client's age, cultural influences, and community to reflect scenarios the client may actually experience. Each index card should have one situation written on it. If desired, the word "Treat," "Sticker," or a smiley face can be written on several cards. During the course of play, if a player selects one of these cards, he or she wins a treat, sticker, or other small prize. Although this is an optional part of the intervention, the prospect of "winning" something during the course of the activity may lower defenses and incorporates an additional component of playfulness to the technique.

In addition to writing the scenarios on the index cards, the therapist draws a happy face and writes "Good Time" on one sheet of paper and a neutral face with the words "Time to Wait" on the other. The papers are hung on opposite walls or in a manner that separates the two concepts.

The session begins with the therapist discussing the importance of addressing problems and processing these issues in therapy as well as appropriately with others who can offer support and guidance. However, clients sometimes struggle to differentiate between circumstances in which talking about the problem may be helpful and times in which it might be best to refrain from discussing the problem. The client is told this activity will help them learn to discriminate between these types of situations.

During the game, players take turns selecting cards, determining whether the situation is a time in which discussing the identified problem is appropriate or whether it is a time in which the client should wait, and then explain why he or she reached that particular decision. The card is then taped onto the corresponding paper, which identifies the situation as either a "Good Time" or a "Time to Wait."

To assist the client in understanding this concept, the therapist should select the first card and verbalize his or her thought process out loud while determining whether the situation written on the card is a good time to discuss the identified problem or a time to wait. For example, the therapist's verbalizations for the scenario "on the playground with all the other kids," might go something like this: "If I discuss this on the playground with all the other kids around, they may not understand the situation so they probably won't be able to help me. Also, some of the kids might repeat my problem or even tease me about it. So, based on this, *on the playground with all the other kids*' is probably a time when it won't help me to talk about the problem so I think I should wait." By verbalizing this thought process, the therapist provides the client with information pertaining to assessing interpersonal boundaries in regard to discussing private, sensitive information with others.

Sometimes, practitioners struggle with this intervention because they feel the intervention gives the covert message that the client should be ashamed of the problem they are facing. On the contrary, this intervention focuses on the problem being private and involving information for which the client deserves support from individuals who are willing, able, and in a position to support and provide help to the client. The emphasis of the intervention is on privacy, not on secrecy. Comparing the problem to other private topics might help explain this concept to young children. For example, underwear is a private topic. Explaining to a young child that although we don't have to be ashamed of our underwear, on the same token, we don't need to talk about our underwear with everyone either.

Although this intervention can be utilized across populations for a variety of sensitive issues and topics, it is particularly useful for sexually abused children since societal misconceptions and misunderstandings about sexual victimization often result in victims being isolated or rejected when they discuss their abuse.

"*Good Time*" scenarios for Who, What, Where, and When

- Alone with my teacher

- With a doctor or nurse

- With a social worker

- With a counselor

- In group counseling

- In therapy

- Alone with my best friend *(Note: This scenario should be thoroughly processed with the client as this situation can fall into either category)*

- Alone with someone I trust in my family

"*Time to Wait*" scenarios for Who, What, Where, and When

- On the playground with all the other kids

- On the school bus

- In line at the grocery store

- With a stranger

- With someone I just met

- At the babysitter's with all the other kids

- In the bathroom at school

- At a birthday party

Chapter 7: Sexual Abuse

Sexual abuse transcends all cultural, ethnic, and socioeconomic boundaries and constitutes a significant social problem. It is impossible to overstate the tragic consequences endured by children, adolescents, and families impacted by sexual abuse. Subsequently, it is imperative that professionals providing treatment to victims of sexual abuse and their families have effective interventions as part of their practice.

This chapter provides participants with play therapy interventions that have practical implications for work with victims of sexual abuse. Techniques focus on reframing distorted cognitions of guilt, blame, and responsibility and understanding the element of secrecy inherent in many cases of sexual abuse.

The interventions contained in this chapter are trauma-focused and directive techniques to create structure and address specific clinical issues related to sexual victimization. However, they are also engaging and playful to aid in lowering avoidance and providing emotional safety. A combination of these therapeutic elements contributes to optimal circumstances in which children might address their posttraumatic issues.

Twisted Thinking

Intervention Summary

Cognitive-behavioral therapy is grounded in the interdependence of cognitions, emotions, and behavior with the basic premise of identifying and altering maladaptive beliefs and replacing them with more adaptive ones. This cognitive-behavioral technique uses the game Twister™ (Milton Bradley) as a format to identify and reframe distorted cognitions of guilt, blame, and responsibility for sexual abuse. Common distorted cognitions of guilt, blame, and responsibility are written on the Twister™ mat and corresponding reframes are written on circles that coincide with the color of the distorted cognitions on the mat. Players take turns spinning the Twister™ spinner and locating the reframe for each of the distorted cognitions written on the mat.

Purpose

- Identify and reframe distorted cognitions of guilt, blame, and responsibility related to sexual abuse
- Reinforce that the client is not responsible for sexual abuse
- Empowerment

Modality

- Individual
- Group
- Family

Age Range

- 8 years–Adult

Materials

- Twister™ (Milton Bradley)
- Permanent black marker
- Scotch tape
- Circle cutter

- Colored cardstock (red, green, blue, yellow)
- Small candy (Jolly Ranchers™, Hershey Kisses™, etc.) or stickers (optional)

Description

Victims of sexual abuse frequently struggle with distorted cognitions of guilt, blame, and responsibility for their victimization. These cognitions are often overtly or covertly reinforced by others. Children and adolescents often come to believe these thoughts and struggle to reframe them without assistance. Assessing, processing, and reframing these distorted thoughts of guilt, blame, and responsibility are a cornerstone of treatment with victims of sexual abuse. This intervention focuses on identifying and reframing common distorted thoughts of guilt, blame, and responsibility and provides a foundation for future therapeutic work to assess the client's specific thoughts regarding guilt, blame, and responsibility.

This technique is a modified version of the game Twister™ (Milton Bradley). Prior to the session, the therapist uses the black permanent marker to write different distorted cognitions of guilt, blame, and responsibility for sexual abuse on the circles of the Twister™ mat. A list of possible distorted cognitions is included on the following pages to serve as a guide. The Twister™ mat consists of four rows of circles arranged according to color. There are six circles in each row. Of the six circles, the therapist writes distorted cognitions on four of the circles. The remaining two circles in the row are labeled with a smiley face. During the game, players that reveal the smiley face select a sticker, treat, or small prize. Although this is an optional part of the intervention, the prospect of earning something during the course of the activity may lower defenses and incorporates an additional component of playfulness to the game.

After the distorted cognitions are written on the mat, the therapist uses the circle cutter and cardstock to create covers for the mat. The color of the covers should correspond with the color of the circle on the mat (i.e. green circles on the mat are covered using the green cardstock; red circles are covered using the red cardstock, etc.). It is recommended that the covers be laminated for durability. The covers are taped over the circles on the Twister™ mat to cover the distorted cognitions written on the mat.

Next, the therapist cuts circles out of the cardstock to create reframes for each distorted cognition. The color selected for each reframe should correspond to the color of the distorted cognition (i.e. the reframe for a green distorted cognition is written on a green circle, the reframe for a red distorted cognition is written on a red circle, etc.). After the reframes are written on the circles, it is recommended that the circles be laminated for durability.

Prior to the session, the Twister™ mat is hung securely on the wall using masking tape. Each circle on the mat should be covered to hide the distorted cognition. The reframes are grouped by color and spread out on a table, floor, or other flat surface.

During the game, players take turns spinning the Twister™ spinner and removing a corresponding cover from the mat. (Note: If the spinner lands on a color and all the covers have been removed, the player spins again.) After the cover is removed, the player reads the distorted cognition and selects the corresponding reframe from among the reframed circles. The selected reframe is taped over the distorted cognition. If the player removes a cover and a smiley face is revealed, the player selects a piece of candy. Stickers can be used instead of candy if desired. Again, this optional component of the intervention may lower defenses and creates an additional level of playfulness.

Reframing distorted cognitions of guilt, blame, and responsibility is a very difficult process for victims of sexual abuse. Since the reframes for this intervention are written on the same color as the distorted cognitions, the reframe is easier to locate. Throughout the activity, clients are encouraged to discuss their own experience regarding thoughts of guilt, blame, and responsibility. Thoughts and feelings regarding the reframed cognitions are processed in relation to each client's experience as well.

The list of potential distorted cognitions and corresponding reframes included in this book is intended to serve as a guide for the therapist. This list is not exhaustive and should be modified to reflect the treatment needs of the client.

Distorted Cognitions and Reframes for "Twisted Thinking"

- I should have told sooner.

  I didn't tell sooner because I was scared and confused.

- I should have said "no."

  I couldn't say "no" because the abuser was someone I trusted.

- It's my fault because I kept the abuse a secret.

  I kept the abuse a secret because I was worried what would happen if I told.

- It is my fault because my family is upset with me.

  People can have their own feelings. It's not my fault if people are upset.

- It's my fault because I knew no one was supposed to touch my private parts.

  Even if I knew my private parts weren't supposed to be touched, I couldn't stop the sexual abuse because I was scared and didn't know what to do.

- It's my fault my family broke up after I told about the sexual abuse.

  My family broke up because the abuser hurt me and committed a crime.

- It's my fault because I shouldn't have trusted the abuser.

  I was tricked into trusting the abuser.

- I feel guilty because the abuser got in trouble after I told.

  The abuser got into trouble because they committed a crime, not because I told.

- I think it's my fault because I touched the abuser too.

  I was tricked into touching the abuser.

- I think the abuse is my fault because I didn't tell the abuser to stop.

   I didn't tell the abuser to stop because I was being tricked into going along with the sexual abuse.

- I think the sexual abuse is my fault because I am a bad kid.

   Nobody deserves to be sexually abused because of the way they act. I am important and deserve to be taken care of.

- It is my fault because sometimes my body felt good when it was being touched.

   Some parts of my body are supposed to feel good when they are touched. That doesn't mean the sexual abuse is my fault.

- I think the abuse is my fault because I took gifts and treats from the abuser.

   The abuser tricked me by giving me gifts and treats so I would keep the sexual abuse a secret.

- I made the sexual abuse happen because I wore sexy clothes.

   Nothing I wore caused the sexual abuse. The abuser is the one who caused the abuse.

- I think the abuse is my fault because I liked being treated special by the abuser.

   I deserve to be treated special. Treating me special did not give the abuser the right to hurt me.

- I think the abuse is my fault because I had to go to a foster home after I told.

   I had to go to a foster home to keep me safe, not because I did something wrong.

Note: The activity "Guilt Trip" from Paper Dolls and Paper Airplanes (Lay, Lowenstein, & Crisci, 1998) served as a guide to develop the distorted cognitions and corresponding reframes for the intervention "Twisted Thinking."

Healing the Hurt

Intervention Summary

This cognitive-behavioral technique, in which maladaptive cognitions are refuted and replaced with more adaptive cognitions, focuses on identifying and reframing clients' specific distorted cognitions of guilt, blame, and responsibility related to the sexual abuse. Distorted cognitions of guilt, blame, and responsibility for sexual abuse are written inside "injuries" using the "invisible" marker from a package of Crayola Color Changeable Markers™. Corresponding reframes for these "injuries" are created during the course of the activity and written on large band-aids. During the game, players take turns coloring an injury with a Color Changeable Marker™ and healing the "injury" by covering the distorted cognition with the corresponding band-aid reframe.

Purpose

- Identify and reframe distorted cognitions of guilt, blame, and responsibility for sexual abuse
- Reinforce the child/adolescent is not responsible for the sexual abuse
- Empowerment

Modality

- Individual
- Group
- Family

Age Range

- 8 years–Adult

Materials

- Flip chart or paper with a large heart drawn on it
- Crayola Color Changeable Markers™
- Extra large band-aids (the type for large injuries)
- Candy/stickers (optional)

Description

Victims of sexual abuse frequently struggle with distorted cognitions of guilt, blame, and responsibility for their victimization. These cognitions are often either overtly or covertly reinforced by others who make statements that allude to victims being responsible for the abuse. These statements include such things as "Why didn't you tell sooner?" or "You know no one is supposed to touch your private parts." Some children and adolescents may hold deep-seated beliefs in distorted thoughts regarding guilt, blame, and responsibility and may need assistance in reframing these misattributions. Subsequently, assessing, processing, and reframing these thoughts are a cornerstone of treatment with victims of sexual abuse. This intervention focuses on identifying and reframing the specific distorted thoughts of guilt, blame, and responsibility each client is struggling with.

Prior to the session, the therapist draws a large heart on the flip chart. Inside the heart, the therapist draws shapes to represent different "injuries." Inside the "injuries," the therapist uses the invisible marker from the Crayola Color Changeables™ to write various distorted cognitions related to guilt, blame, and responsibility for sexual abuse. A guideline of distorted cognitions can be obtained from the previous activity, "Twisted Thinking." However, the purpose of this intervention is to elicit and reframe the client's specific distorted cognitions. This can be accomplished by either asking the client directly about distorted thoughts related to guilt, blame, and responsibility or by using clinical information that alludes to possible distorted cognitions. For example, a distorted cognition for a female client whose mother stated during the assessment interview, "I don't understand why she didn't tell sooner," might be "I feel like the sexual abuse is my fault because I didn't tell sooner." When the distorted cognitions are written using the invisible marker, the "injuries" will look blank.

During the course of the activity, the therapist and client will collaboratively challenge and process the distorted cognitions and generate more adaptive reframes for the cognitions. These reframes will be written on the large band-aids. After the reframe is written, the band-aid is used to cover and "heal" the painful distorted thought of guilt, blame, and responsibility.

The activity begins by discussing the fact that victims of sexual abuse often feel responsible for their victimization. As a result, their hearts are hurt and filled with feelings of guilt, blame, and responsibility. This activity will help "heal" the hurt.

During the activity, players take turns coloring in an "injury" with the Color Changeable Markers™. Coloring in the "injury" will reveal the distorted cognition previously written with the invisible marker. After the "injury" has been revealed, the distorted cognition is processed, challenged for its validity, and then collaboratively reframed with a more accurate, adaptive cognition. The reframe is written on a band-aid that is placed over the injury (distorted cognition), thereby healing the hurt caused by the distorted cognition.

If desired, the therapist can draw a smiley face inside some "injuries." When a player colors in an injury and a smiley face is revealed, the player selects a small piece of candy, sticker, or small prize. Although this is optional, the prospect of "winning" a piece of candy, sticker, or small prize serves to lower defenses and incorporates a component of fun and playfulness into the activity.

Throughout the activity, clients discuss their experience regarding cognitions pertaining to guilt, blame, and responsibility for the sexual abuse. Thoughts and feelings regarding the reframed cognitions are processed in relation to the client's experience as well.

One of the distinct advantages of this intervention is that it focuses on the specific distorted cognitions of each client and is modified to reflect the clinical needs of each individual.

It's Not that Simple

Intervention Summary

This intervention acknowledges and explores the element of secrecy inherent in many cases of sexual abuse and normalizes reasons why victims are often unable to readily disclose sexual abuse. A small magnet represents the client, a large magnet symbolizes help and protection from the abuse, and Play-Doh® serves as reasons why victims do not disclose the abuse. During the course of the activity, pieces of Play-Doh® are squished around the small magnet to represent various reasons the client did not disclose the abuse. When "help and protection" are finally made available, the Play-Doh® has created a barrier between the small magnet and the "help." This serves to represent how barriers and obstacles made it difficult to disclose the abuse. The barriers are then removed to symbolize the client's ability to disclose the abuse despite the various obstacles and to support and validate the client's disclosure.

Purpose

- Develop an understanding of the secrecy inherent in many cases of sexual abuse
- Normalize obstacles to disclosure
- Reinforce the child/adolescent is not responsible for the sexual abuse
- Empowerment

Modality

- Individual
- Group
- Family

Age Range

- 8 years–Adults

Materials

- Marble magnets (Discount School Supply) or another type of small magnet
- Large Horseshoe Magnet (Discount School Supply) or another large magnet
- Play-Doh® (Hasbro)

Description

One of the first reactions children may receive when they disclose sexual abuse is "Why didn't you tell me?" or "How come you didn't tell sooner?" These types of statements place blame onto the child and do not acknowledge and validate the dynamics of sexual abuse and the inherent element of secrecy in many sexually abusive situations. Unfortunately, there is a societal misconception that children who are sexually abused can merely say "no" or immediately disclose the abuse. This is compounded by the fact that children are usually socialized to learn that no one is supposed to touch their private parts. However, sexual abuse is not that simple. There are many factors that create obstacles for disclosure. This activity examines these barriers, normalizes their existence, and provides an understanding of how these factors interfere with disclosure.

In the intervention, the small marble magnet represents the client, the large horseshoe magnet represents "help," and the Play-Doh® represents the various reasons clients are not able to readily disclose sexual abuse.

The client selects a small colored marble to represent him or her. The therapist tells the client that people are often faced with problems or situations in which they need to get help. For this technique, the large horseshoe magnet symbolizes various sources of "help." The therapist begins by giving the client several problem situations and asks the client how the client would get help for each situation. After the client identifies who could help in the situation or how they would access help, the large horseshoe magnet is given to the client and the client uses the larger magnet to get "help" (i.e. the client brings the large magnet close to the small magnet, creating a magnetic attraction to symbolize the child getting help for the identified situation).

For example, a possible problem scenario could be: "You wake up in the morning feeling sick. Who can help you?" Possible solutions to this problem might be a parent, a nurse, or a doctor. Once the client identifies a source of help, the client is given the large "helper" magnet and is instructed to get help for his or her smaller magnet. With the client's small magnet resting on a flat surface, the client brings the large "helper" magnet close to the smaller magnet, creating a magnetic attraction in which the small magnet is readily drawn to the larger magnet and attaches to the "help."

A list of possible problem situations is listed on the next page. Clients should be given several problem situations to identify who could help them or how they can get help. For each situation, the horseshoe magnet is given to the client for help to be obtained.

104

The therapist discusses the fact that although there are many situations in which it is easy to get help, sexual abuse is a situation in which it may be very difficult to get help. There are many reasons why children and adolescents struggle to disclose sexual abuse including the fact that sexual abuse often involves secrecy, enticement, and other dynamics that create barriers to disclosure. This activity will explore some of the reasons kids are not able to disclose sexual abuse and how these factors create barriers to receiving help.

The client is given a container of Play-Doh® and directed to roll the Play-Doh® into medium-sized balls (minimum of ten). The client is told the Play-Doh® symbolizes different reasons kids may struggle to tell someone about the sexual abuse. The client is asked to think about and identify some of the reasons he or she was unable to disclose the abuse. If needed, the therapist can provide some common reasons that create barriers and obstacles to readily disclose sexual abuse. A list of possible reasons is listed on the next page. These reasons include such things as feeling scared, not wanting the abuser to get into trouble, or thinking they will get in trouble if they tell.

For each reason identified, the client squishes a ball of Play-Doh® onto the magnet. The client continues to generate reasons until the entire magnet is covered with Play-Doh®.

As the client identifies various reasons, the therapist normalizes the reasons and expresses an understanding of how the reasons create barriers to disclosing the abuse.

Once the marble is covered with reasons that make it difficult to readily disclose the sexual abuse, the client is given the large "helper" magnet. The client is reminded the large magnet represents "help," and in this situation, the large magnet symbolizes getting "help" to end the sexual abuse. This help can be the non-offending parent, a family member, a teacher, a neighbor, the police, or another trusted adult who can protect the client from the abuse. The client is given the large magnet and instructed to get help to end the sexual abuse. However, no matter how close the large magnet is brought to the small magnet, the two magnets will be unable to connect because the reasons the child struggled to disclose the abuse (i.e. the Play-Doh®) have created a barrier in between the client (small magnet) and the help the client needs (large magnet). Subsequently, the dynamic of secrecy inherent in sexually abusive situations is symbolically represented, acknowledged, and normalized.

When the horseshoe magnet and the marble magnet do not successfully connect, the therapist processes this by making a statement such as, "I wonder why the small magnet is not getting help?" The fact that the small magnet cannot get help because the Play-Doh® is getting in the way is then processed. The reasons children and adolescents do not tell about sexual abuse are normalized and validated. The client is told that, under these circumstances, it is understandable that the client was not able to readily disclose the sexual abuse. Delayed disclosure does not make the sexual abuse the child's responsibility, but is a reflection of the secrecy and dynamics of sexual abuse itself.

A discussion ensues regarding all of the obstacles and barriers the client had to overcome in order to disclose and/or discuss the sexual abuse. The Play-Doh® is then removed to symbolize the client breaking free of these barriers to begin their journey of healing. The client's courage is recognized, validated, and supported and the disclosure of the sexual abuse is reframed as an act of bravery.

This intervention provides a concrete representation of reasons why victims of sexual abuse are not able to readily disclose their abuse and the barrier these reasons create in regard to accessing help and protection and ending the abuse. Not only is this intervention helpful for victims of sexual abuse, it is also very powerful for the non-offending parent and other family members in understanding that it is not that simple for victims to disclose sexual abuse.

Problem Situations for "It's Not that Simple"

- You wake up sick in the morning.
- You are lost in a large store.
- Someone at school is teasing you.
- You missed the school bus at the end of the day.
- You arrive at school and realize you forgot your lunch.
- You are trying to do your homework but don't understand it.
- You are being threatened by a bully.
- You are having a fight with your best friend.

Reasons Kids Don't Tell

- I was scared.
- I was confused.
- I didn't want the abuser to get in trouble.
- I didn't know who to tell.
- I thought the abuse was my fault.
- I was too overwhelmed.
- I thought I would get in trouble.
- I was ashamed.
- I was embarrassed.
- I didn't think anyone would believe me.
- I thought people would think the abuse was my fault.
- I worried what people would think about me if they knew what was happening.
- I felt guilty.
- I was worried about what would happen if I told.
- I didn't want to upset my mom.
- I felt hopeless, like no one would be able to help me.
- I didn't want to break up my family.
- I was afraid I'd get taken away.

- My family needed the abuser.

- I was afraid the abuser would hurt me.

- I was afraid the abuser would hurt someone in my family.

- I felt too alone to tell anyone.

- I didn't think people would understand.

- Because I didn't say "no," I thought people would blame me.

- Because I didn't tell sooner, I felt like it was my fault.

- I didn't tell because I thought I was "letting" him abuse me, making the abuse my fault too.

Chapter 8: Termination

Termination is an essential, but often overlooked, phase of treatment. During the process of termination, interventions should focus on reviewing and strengthening skills acquired in treatment, exploring the use of acquired skills in the client's future, and facilitating closure on the therapeutic relationship.

Interventions in this chapter contain techniques that address these areas, instill hope, and are future-oriented. Use of these tools will help prepare children, adolescents, and families for termination while honoring the sensitive process of closure. The play-based approach of the following interventions is consistent with previous techniques presented in this manual to place closure on the treatment process as children, adolescents, and families prepare for the next phase of their lives.

During the termination phase, other interventions from this manual can be repeated with an emphasis on supporting use of the therapeutic skills and focusing on the individual's progress and growth. For example, the technique "Revealing Your Feelings" from the chapter on Emotional Expression can be repeated during the termination stage with an emphasis on processing emotions related to termination of therapy and the client's future.

Farewell Fortune Cookies

Intervention Summary

To facilitate healthy closure and termination, therapeutic questions related to termination are presented to the client for review and discussion. Topics for questions include reviewing skills acquired in therapy, placing closure on the therapeutic relationship, and instilling hope for the future. Questions are written and taped on the outside of individually wrapped fortune cookies. Players take turns selecting a "farewell fortune cookie" and responding to the corresponding therapeutic question.

Purpose

- Facilitate termination of therapy
- Facilitate emotional expression regarding termination
- Facilitate closure of the therapeutic relationship
- Emphasize and review therapeutic gains
- Support generalization
- Focus on the client's future
- Instill hope

Modality

- Individual
- Group
- Family

Age Range

- 5 years–Adults

Materials

- Fortune cookies
- Therapeutic questions (see attached)

Description

Termination is an important aspect of therapy and warrants individual, clinical attention. As therapy comes to a close, techniques should emphasize processing emotions relating to termination as well as reviewing therapeutic gains and focusing on the future (Jones, Robinson, & Casado, 2003). This technique utilizes the symbolism and metaphor of fortune cookies to focus on the client's future, instill hope, explore and review the therapeutic process, and support closure of the therapeutic relationship.

Prior to the session, the therapist purchases fortune cookies. Fortune cookies can be purchased at most grocery stores in the oriental food section. If possible, individually wrapped cookies should be purchased. Therapeutic questions are written on strips of paper, which are folded and taped onto the outside of each individual cookie. If cookies are not individually wrapped, the therapeutic questions can be rolled up and inserted inside the fortune cookie using a pair of tweezers. In the latter case, clients will have two fortunes inside each cookie - one traditional fortune and one "therapeutic" fortune.

During the activity, players take turns selecting a "farewell fortune cookie" and responding to the corresponding therapeutic question. If this intervention is utilized in individual therapy, the client and therapist take turns selecting farewell fortune cookies and responding to the therapeutic questions. If utilized in group or family therapy, the therapist has the option of participating in the technique or serving only as a facilitator.

The therapeutic questions for this intervention focus on different aspects of the termination process. Questions were formulated based on clinical literature that delineates tasks appropriate for the termination stage of treatment including such things as therapeutic closure, exploring the future, reviewing therapeutic gains, and preparing the client for termination of therapy (Jones, Robinson, & Casado, 2003). The questions provided for this technique are intended to serve as a clinical guide and should be modified for the individual needs of each client.

Clients may be tempted to eat several fortune cookies during the intervention. Since eating more then a few cookies is not advisable, limits with regard to eating the cookies should be established at the onset of the activity. Establishing a simple limit such as permitting the client to take extra cookies home may address this issue.

Questions for Farewell Fortune Cookies

- What is one mistake from your past you have learned from?

- What is one goal you have for the future and how will you reach it?

- What is one thing you have learned in therapy?

- Name one person you can turn to for support/help.

- What type of family do you see yourself having in the future?

- What job do you want to have and what steps will you take to get that job?

- What qualities do you have that will help you succeed in the future?

- What is one activity or hobby you enjoy that helps you cope with stress?

- Where do you see yourself in ten years?

- What is something you enjoy that you might be able to use in a career?

- What is something you will miss about therapy?

- What is something you won't miss about therapy?

- What is one problem or obstacle you have overcome?

- How do you feel about ending therapy?

- How can you use what you've learned in therapy in your future?

Our Good-Bye, Hello Card

Intervention Summary

This intervention explores termination as a parallel process of both a closure and a beginning. To create a memento of this process, the client and therapist collaboratively create a card that symbolizes the closure of therapy on the outside of the card and acknowledges and welcomes the next chapter of the client's life post-termination on the inside of the card.

Purpose

- Facilitate termination of therapy
- Facilitate emotional expression regarding termination
- Facilitate closure of the therapeutic relationship
- Emphasize and review therapeutic gains
- Support generalization
- Focus on the client's future
- Instill hope

Modality

- Individual
- Group
- Family

Age Range

- 5 years–Adults

Materials

- Design Your Own! Photo Cards by Hands On Fun™ (Oriental Trading Company)
- Cardstock or construction paper
- Drawing and art materials

- Polaroid™ camera or photograph of the client and therapist
- Tape

Preparation

Prior to the session, a photograph of the therapist and child is taken and developed. As an alternative, a Polaroid™ picture can be taken.

Description

Termination is an important aspect of therapy and warrants individual, clinical attention. As therapy comes to a close, techniques should emphasize processing emotions relating to termination as well as reviewing therapeutic gains and focusing on the future (Jones, Robinson, & Casado, 2003). The metaphor for this intervention comes from the fact that termination is both an ending as well as a beginning. In addition to communicating this concept and addressing the aforementioned clinical areas, this technique also provides a transitional object to serve as a memento of the therapeutic relationship.

In this intervention, a card symbolizing closure of therapy as well as the new beginning in the client's life is created collaboratively by the client and therapist. The Design Your Own! Photo Cards by Hands On Fun™ can be purchased from Oriental Trading Company. These cards have a pre-cut center for the photograph of the client and therapist and are made of white cardstock, which can be drawn on using regular markers and drawing supplies. If more economically feasible, regular cardstock or construction paper can be used as an alternative.

The photograph provides a concrete representation of the therapeutic relationship and is placed in the center of the "good-bye, hello" card.

During the session, the therapist and client design the "good-bye, hello" card to place closure on the therapeutic relationship while acknowledging the new beginning in the client's life. The therapist explains termination as being a "good-bye" to therapy and a "hello" to a new part of life, hence the name of the technique. To communicate this, a "good-bye, hello" card will be created by the client and therapist, which will contain both elements of closure as well as elements of welcoming or greeting. The outside of the card should be designed using symbols, pictures, or words reminiscent of therapy. For example, a drawing of two stick figures can represent the therapist and child working together or a picture of different feeling faces can represent the fact that the child learned to talk about their feelings.

The inside of the card should be decorated with symbols, pictures, and words that represent the client's future. In addition, a message that focuses on memories of therapy and the therapeutic relationship as well as hopes, plans, and dreams regarding the client's future is written collaboratively by the client and therapist. Feelings about termination and a review of the progress made in therapy can also be incorporated into the message. For younger children, sentence stems can be provided to serve as a foundation for the message. Potential sentence stems include: "When I think about therapy ending, I feel…," "One thing I learned in therapy that will help me is…," "The skill I learned in therapy I use the most is…," and "In my future…" The written message creates an opportunity to provide recognition and praise for the client's progress as well as encouragement for their future.

One of the distinct advantages of this intervention is that it provides a transitional object and memento of therapy. For clients in the foster care system who have experienced significant loss, this keepsake is particularly helpful.

Lifesavers

Intervention Summary

As termination of therapy proceeds, clients' connection to their support system should be acknowledged and strengthened. For this activity, Lifesaver™ candies are used to represent traits, qualities, and characteristics the client finds helpful during times of need. Individuals in the client's support system who provide these qualities are identified with an emphasis on the client using support from these individuals post-termination to maintain therapeutic gains.

Purpose

- Identify the client's support system
- Strengthen the client's connection with his or her support system
- Identify ways the client can utilize his or her support system following termination
- Facilitate termination of therapy
- Facilitate closure of the therapeutic relationship
- Focus on the client's future
- Instill hope

Modality

- Individual
- Group
- Family

Age Range

- 11–18 years

Materials

- Cardstock or construction paper
- Lifesavers™ candy

- Glue

- Markers

Description

As therapy comes to a close, it is essential to not only place closure on the therapeutic relationship, but to also strengthen clients' connection with their support system. This intervention provides clarification of people in the client's support system and identifies ways this support system can be utilized by the client.

The intervention is divided into two parts. During the first part, the client identifies qualities that the client finds helpful and supportive in times of need. During the second part of the intervention, the client identifies individuals in his or her life who provide the identified qualities. The concept of a lifesaver provides the underlying metaphor for the technique as lifesavers provide lifesaving support during dire times. This concept is explained to the client. The statement "You're such a lifesaver" and the use of lifesavers as flotation devices can be discussed as well.

The importance of the client seeking and utilizing support from the lifesavers in his or her support system after therapy ends is discussed with an emphasis placed on how this support will help the client sustain the changes and gains the client has acquired through treatment. However, before seeking support, clients need to understand what type of support they need since different people find different qualities helpful during times of need. If necessary, the therapist can provide examples of this such as how some people may be seeking advice from individuals in their support system whereas other people might be seeking someone to merely listen to them.

The client and therapist brainstorm a list of qualities that might be helpful during times of need. As qualities are identified, they are written to create a list of potential qualities. This list can be utilized by the client as needed. A list of possible qualities is included on the following pages to serve as a guide for this process. Concepts included on this list may need to be defined for younger children.

Once a list of helpful qualities is generated, the client uses the list to select approximately four to seven qualities that he or she finds helpful during difficult times. For each quality identified, the client selects a Lifesaver™ candy, glues the candy onto the card stock, and labels the Lifesaver™ with the corresponding quality.

Once the qualities are identified and the Lifesavers™ are glued onto the card stock and labeled, the client is challenged to think about individuals in his or her life who provide the qualities identified. Lifesavers™ are labeled with the corresponding names of those individuals. The "lifesavers" can have more then one individual associated with them. If clients have identified a quality but don't know who in their life can provide that quality, this area is processed. Since the primary focus of this intervention is to identify and strengthen clients' connection to their support system in preparation for termination of the therapeutic relationship, if clients cannot identify someone who provides a quality for them, another quality can be identified.

A modification of this intervention would be for the client to label the Lifesavers™ as significant individuals in his or her life and then list the qualities each individual provides for the client.

This intervention can be as creative or simple as clinically appropriate. With some clients, the metaphor of lifesavers as flotation devices can be employed and the client can draw a boat and water on the cardstock before the "lifesavers" are glued on. If this analogy is used, as an additional component, anchors can be drawn at the bottom of the page to represent qualities the child finds unhelpful. For example, an individual who does not want advice during times of need can place an anchor labeled "advice" at the bottom of his or her activity. For an individual who needs personal space during difficult times, nurturing, physical contact, or hugs might be an identified anchor.

Since termination removes the practitioner as a member of the client's support system, use of this intervention during the ending stage of treatment provides a structured, developmentally-appropriate way to explore and strengthen clients' connection with other individuals in their support system.

Clients may be tempted to eat several Lifesavers™ candies while completing this activity. Since eating too many candies is not advisable, limits with regard to eating the Lifesavers™ should be established at the onset of the activity. Limiting the amount of candy that can be eaten during the session and/or permitting clients to take some Lifesavers™ home with them might address this issue.

Possible Helpful Qualities for "Lifesavers"

- Good listener

- Advice

- Physical touch / TLC / Hugs

- Nurturing

- Praise

- Encouragement

- Patience

- Humor

- Understanding

- Compassion

- Comfort

- Companionship

- Silence

- Someone to let me vent

- Someone to have fun with

- Supportive

- Inspirational

- Gentle

- Calm

- Optimistic

- Hopeful

References

American Psychiatric Association. (2000). *Diagnostic and statistical manual of mental disorders* (4th ed., text rev.). Washington, DC: Author.

Deblinger, E. & Heflin, A.H. (1996). *Treating sexually abused children and their nonoffending parents: A cognitive behavioral approach.* Thousand Oaks, CA: Sage Publications.

Gil, E. (2006). *Helping abused and traumatized children: Integrating directive and nondirective approaches.* New York: The Guilford Press.

Gil, E. (2007). *Connecting with families using creativity in play: Assessment and treatment ideas.* Keynote address presented at the Texas Association for Play Therapy 14th Annual Play Therapy Conference. El Paso, TX: Unpublished presentation.

Jones, K.D., Casado, M., & Robinson, E.H. (2003). Structured play therapy: A model for choosing topics & activities. *International Journal of Play Therapy, 12*(1), 31-47.

Knell, S. (1983). *Cognitive behavioral play therapy.* Northvale, NJ: Jason Aronson.

Lay, M., Lowenstein, L., & Crisci, G. (1998). *Paper dolls and paper airplanes: Therapeutic activities for sexually traumatized children.* Charlotte, NC: Kidsrights.

Reddy, L.A., Files-Hall, T.M., & Schaefer, C.E. (Eds.). (2005). *Empirically based play interventions for children.* Washington, DC: American Psychological Association.

Rev, J.M., Schrader, E., & Morris-Yates, A. (1992). Parent-child agreement on children's behaviors reported by the Child Behavior Checklist (CBCL). *Journal of Adolescence, 15,* 219-230.

Roberts, A.R., & Yeager, K.R. (Eds.). (2006). *Foundations of evidence-based social work practice.* New York: Oxford University Press.

Saunders, B.E., Berliner, L., & Hanson, R.F. (Eds.). (2004). *Child physical and sexual abuse: Guidelines for treatment* (Revised Report: April 26, 2004). Charleston, SC: National Crime Victims Research and Treatment Center.

Schaefer, C.E. (2001). Prescriptive play therapy. *International Journal of Play Therapy, 10*(2), 57-73.

Shelby, J.S., & Felix, E.D. (2005). Posttraumatic play therapy: The need for an integrated model of directive and nondirective approaches. In L.A. Reddy, T.M. Files-Hall, & C.E. Schaefer (Eds.), *Empirically based play interventions for children.* Washington, DC: American Psychological Association.

Sheppard, C.H. (1998). *Brave bart: A story for traumatized and grieving children.* Grosse Pointe Woods, MI: Institute for Trauma and Loss in Children.

Resources & Materials

Anna's Toy Depot

1-888-227-9169

www.annastoydepot.com

Child Craft

1-800-631-5652

www.childcraft.com

Childswork Childsplay

1-800-962-1141

www.childswork.com

Crayola

1-800-CRAYOLA

www.crayola.com

Discount School Supply

1-800-627-2829

www.DiscountSchoolSupply.com

Macro Products Inc

1-800-448-2197

www.macroproducts.com

Oriental Trading Co.

1-800-228-2269

www.orientaltrading.com

Rose Play Therapy Toys

www.roseplaytherapy.com

S & S Worldwide

1-800-243-9232

www.ssww.com

Self-Esteem Shop

1-800-251-8336

www.selfesteemshop.com

Uniquity

1-800-521-7771

Professional Associations & Resources

Play Therapy

- Association for Play Therapy (www.a4pt.org)
- British Association of Play Therapists (www.bapt.info)
- Canadian Play Therapy Association (www.cacpt.com)
- Center for Play Therapy (www.coe.unt.edu/cpt)
- International Society for Child and Play Therapy (www.playtherapy.org)

Professional Links

- American Art Therapy Association, Inc (www.arttherapy.org)
- American Association for Marriage & Family Therapy (www.aamft.org)
- American Psychological Association (www.apa.org)
- National Association of Social Workers (www.socialworkers.org)

Mental Health

- Association for Children's Mental Health (www.acmh-mi.org)
- National Child Traumatic Stress Network (www.nctsnet.org)
- National Institute for Mental Health (www.nimh.nih.gov)
- US Department of Health & Human Services (www.hhs.gov)

Play therapy training, supervision, & consultation are available throughout the United States & abroad. For additional information, please contact:

Sueann Kenney-Noziska, MSW, LCSW, RPT-S

Email:info@playtherapycorner.com

Website: www.playtherapycorner.com

About the Author

Sueann Kenney-Noziska, MSW, LCSW, RPT-S, is a Licensed Clinical Social Worker and Registered Play Therapist Supervisor specializing in using play therapy in clinical practice with children, adolescents, and their families. As part of her clinical work, she provides intensive outpatient mental health services to severe and impoverished children and adolescents and coordinates a sexual abuse treatment program. In addition, Sueann provides case consultation as well as clinical and play therapy supervision.

She is an instructor of play therapy, guest lecturer, and internationally recognized speaker who has trained hundreds of professionals. Sueann is known as a dynamic, engaging presenter with a reputation for providing practical and clinically useful play therapy interventions. Her seminars are consistently rated as "outstanding" and highlight the original play therapy interventions she has contributed to the field.

Sueann is founder and President of Play Therapy Corner, Incorporated, an organization dedicated to supporting and facilitating professional development for counseling and mental health professionals who use play therapy in their clinical practice. In addition, she is actively involved in the play therapy community where she has held several leadership positions including President of the California Association for Play Therapy (CALAPT) and National Committee Chair for the Leadership Academy for the Association for Play Therapy (APT).

Sueann earned her Bachelors of Science in Psychology from the University of South Dakota (1993), Masters of Social Work from San Diego State University (1998), and Specialized Certificate in Play Therapy from the University of California San Diego (2001).